PETS TELL THE TRUTH

A MYSTICAL JOURNEY INTO THE ANIMAL MIND

AGNES JULIA THOMAS, Ph.D
Scientist, Educator and Animal
Telepathic Communicator

GARNETT
PUBLISHING
Cleveland, Ohio

Pets Tell the Truth: A mystical journey into the animal mind.
Copyright © 2005 by Agnes J. Thomas. All rights reserved.

Hanover Publishing Company Inc.
Brecksville, Ohio 44141

First Printing: 2005
Second Printing: 2005
Third Printing: 2008

All photos courtesy of Agnes J. Thomas

Further inquiries to Agnes J. Thomas, Ph.D may be addressed to:
Agnes J. Thomas, Ph.D
7569 Sanctuary Circle
Brecksville, OH 44141
(440)838-0911
talktopets@aol.com

Library of Congress Control Number: 2005931390

ISBN: 978-0-9802411-0-5

"A human being is part of the whole called by us Universe, a part limited in time and space. We experience ourselves, our thoughts and feelings as something separate from the rest. A kind of optical delusion of consciousness. This delusion is a kind of prison for us, restricting us to our personal desires and to affection for a few persons nearest to us. Our task must be to free ourselves from the prison by widening our circle of compassion to embrace all living creatures and the whole of nature in its beauty...We shall require a substantially new manner of thinking if mankind is to survive."

— Albert Einstein

To the reader,

It is with deep humility and respect that I invite you to share in what I consider to be a privileged insight into the mind of animals.

Agnes J. Thomas, Ph.D.

TABLE OF CONTENTS

Preface 8

About the author... 11

Acknowledgements 14

PART ONE

CHAPTER ONE 15
Frosty Introduces Me to Interspecies Telepathic Communication

CHAPTER TWO.. 32
Animals as Fellow Spiritual Beings in Creation

CHAPTER THREE 36
Farm Animals

CHAPTER FOUR 43
The Procedure: How to Communicate with Animals

CHAPTER FIVE.. 50
Wild Animals

CHAPTER SIX 62
Shamanism and Telepathic Communication

PART TWO

CHAPTER SEVEN.. 70
How Animals Think

CHAPTER EIGHT.. 79
Pet Truths

CHAPTER NINE 95
Death and Dying

CHAPTER TEN 116
The Animal Consultation Process

PART THREE

CHAPTER ELEVEN 131
Telepathy: How it Really Works

CHAPTER TWELVE 142
Plants, Trees, Rocks, and Mother Earth

CHAPTER THIRTEEN 151
Animals and Medical Research

CHAPTER FOURTEEN 158
The Healing Power of Animals

CHAPTER FIFTEEN 164
The Big Picture

APPENDIX

Notes 166
References 168
How Animals Think Resources 173

Preface

Since the beginning of mankind's sojourn on this planet, we have asked ourselves, "Where did I come from and why am I here?" The definition of a human as a being consisting of a physical form which is able to move about and interact with the environment is incomplete in its meaning without the inclusion of physical death. Death then is defined as a physical body without the presence of a life force; that is, an invisible energy responsible for animation of the body. This life energy, sometimes called the soul or spirit, has been poorly understood due to the difficulty in finding ways to measure and define it. As such, traditional scientific disciplines have for centuries ignored it and deferred its understanding to religious sources. It has been a quality of "faith" or "belief in God" which allows the intellect of the individual to integrate the known with the unknown and to comfortably deal with aspects of physical existence and its termination in death.

While the biologist has sophisticated tools to examine the body, its tissues, cells, and fluids to the minutest particle, the psychologist must examine the mind and spirit by use of hypothetical constructs and relationships, derived from language, behavior, and intention. The tools of the physiological psychologist have been primarily observation of animal behavior under laboratory conditions. Studies of this kind are customarily used to assess the development of learning and cognition, and to establish a link between brain and behavior. Critical to this scholastic endeavor is the assumption that the mind is in the brain. Evidence for this belief is the observation that both humans and animals who receive various insults to the brain demonstrate cognitive or behavioral deficits. With the help of sophisticated techniques to measure subtle energies in or near living tissue, recent studies have provided evidence that the mind may not be in the brain, with the brain acting as a decoder of energy and information. This suggests that the mind is somewhere else, and that communication with these subtle energies is possible under laboratory conditions.

In this book, I have combined the knowledge and experience I used as a clinical psychologist for brain-damaged individuals and my laboratory research with animals to establish a scientific basis for the investigation of the animal mind by direct telepathic communication with the animals themselves. In order to prevent the inclusion of psychic phenomena with animal telepathy, I found it necessary to establish simple criteria: "If the observed phenomena could be filtered through science, and reproduced in such a way as to be provable, I would accept it as fact." For example, if an individual animal can communicate to me some piece of information, there must be a validation of the information. If, in a telephone consultation, the animal relates that it is sleeping in the owner's closet next to their brown shoes, the owner must validate that it is so. If a dog looks out the front window and sends me a visual image of children playing baseball in the street, then it is my responsibility as a researcher to write down every detail of the scene, and then drive to the dog's location and compare and correlate my list of observations with the actual scene.

In my workshops, students are instructed to ask a single animal the same question and write down their answers. All participants will receive the same answer from the single animal. Then students will be asked to each pick a different animal and ask the same question. About 98% will receive identical answers from their particular animal, and the other 2% will receive an answer that is worded slightly differently but means the same thing. Consider the question, "What makes daytime?" Some 98% of students will telepathically receive the word, "sun," and 2% will receive the answer, "the ball of light in the sky." Data like this is deemed provable and reliable.

Telepathy is a means of thought transfer which can be proven. In contrast, psychic phenomena are completely different. A psychic has the ability to tell the future; a telepath does not. The accuracy of the psychic prediction (whether it turns out to be correct or not) is a function of the current situation. Because the future is not yet written, there are many confounding variables which may enter the path of the prediction and alter the outcome. The accuracy of the telepathic communication is a direct function of the receptivity and knowledge of the communicator. When an animal sends the communicator an impression, it is an expression of everything the animal sees, hears, tastes, smells, and feels at any given moment. The impression must be received by the telepath, filter up through his or her brain, and then be translated into language.

To establish comparative data, I prepared a standard protocol of questions to ask each animal. This provided for observations of individual differences, both within and among species.

Following these simple criteria, I was able to establish reliable data on the animal mind, and as serendipity, I found reliable evidence for the existence of an afterlife and a basis for mysticism itself.

In 1999, I suffered a back injury which required me to retire from the university. I found that the mind never retires and my scientific curiosity took another form. Without the luxury of funding, a formal laboratory and graduate student assistants, I used the scientific method so familiar to me, and made what I believe to be the most valuable discovery of my long scientific career.

My conversations with animals have been nothing less than life-transforming, not only for me, but for the thousands of clients who live with these wonderful animal companions. Understanding the animal mind and communicating on their level is a transcendental leap from the world of judgment, separation and dualities to one of unity consciousness, and a look at a mind without ego constructs.

As one reads through Part One of this book, it is my hope that the reader can experience the sense of awe and wonder I enjoyed when I began my investigative journey into the minds of animals. Part Two describes the actual experience of entering the telepathic field and what can be found there, including comparisons of human versus animal thought processes, certain truths contained in animal's communications, and their understanding of the afterlife. Part Three discusses my own understanding of telepathy, morphogenesis, and the interconnectedness of life as described to me by the animals themselves.

I ask the reader to take a leap of faith and read the book to the end. It is a story of how we relate to each other and the universe itself. It is a story of why we are here, and where evolution is leading us.

Even as a preschooler, animals naturally drew my attention and admiration. My grandmother's farm had many kinds of animals to watch and appreciate. But it was the nickel movies on Saturday afternoons that really opened my eyes and sparked my interest and desire to understand and communicate with animals. Walt Disney's animated cartoons gifted animals individual personalities. These cartoon characters taught me to see animals as fellow beings instead of just Grandma's livestock. I wondered if her farm animals thought like Mickey Mouse and Donald Duck — if they had attachments, relationships, feelings, hopes and dreams.

In kindergarten, my grandmother gave me a kitten. "Fluffy" was the perfect name for this ball of fur, who overwhelmed me with feelings of love and companionship. It was my first experience with such deep feelings of love and also I became aware that this uncensored relationship allowed my creative ideas and dreams to flow. I wondered if Fluffy knew how much I loved him and wished it was possible to know what he was thinking — about anything and everything. One day, Fluffy mysteriously disappeared. Every day after kindergarten, I walked up and down the neighborhood streets in the snow calling for him. Although I never found him, the bond between us continued even into high school. To this day, I know that somehow we are still connected, even though we never saw each other again.

When I was eighteen years old, I married my best friend Bill, who also shared a great love for animals. One of the first things we did was to adopt a kitten. We opened a small business, a beauty salon, and worked together for several years to "get started" before I entered college. Beauty work was not only artistic and fulfilling, but also afforded me the opportunity to know so many women on a social and personal level. I was always a good listener. Coupled with my compassion I was somewhat of a counselor even in those days.

College was an opportunity to study the human psyche. I specialized in physiological psychology. I loved studying the animal mind as well as the human mind. In Psychology 101, the first thing I was surprised to learn is that the world is not as it seems to be. Perception is a product of one's senses, experiences, preferences, and judgments at any given moment. The world is unique to each observer, and is based upon prior conditioning and an individual's unique vantage point. It is simply an illusion or as the Eastern cultures believe, "Maya." It is fascinating and also a little unsettling to realize the world we create from our own perceptions may be quite different from another's.

For me, empirical science offered a solution to this dilemma. Seeking a more concrete approach to learning and memory, I elected to study the functional relationships of brain and mind. My research focused on the many facets of learning in laboratory animals such as rats, mice, hamsters, and guinea pigs. Studies of this kind are used to discover how animals think and acquire knowledge. Then these discoveries are used to make inferences about how humans may do the same, so rehabilitation strategies may be developed. My mentors instructed me to treat all laboratory animals as pets: to hold them, pet them, give treats, talk to them quietly, and treat them with respect.

Following graduation I worked as a counselor for mentally retarded and brain-damaged children and adults. Some time later, after an automobile accident in which I sustained a severe neck injury, I gave up clinical practice and went into research. My studies focused on how baby animals breathe and learn to regulate their breathing during crying, sucking for milk, and sleep. These studies included developmental brain research and the development of the respiratory control system, subjects for which I am nationally recognized.

During this time, an experience changed my life! Frosty, one of my cats, developed a brain tumor and his health dramatically deteriorated. One day, while waiting for Frosty to be released from the veterinary clinic, I walked into a nearby restaurant for a cup of coffee. A copy of the Cleveland *Plain Dealer* newspaper had been left behind on the seat next to me. I picked it up and became fascinated by an article about a woman in New York who could communicate with animals. The article described how she was able to talk telepathically with animals, even across great distances over the phone. I immediately called her. She communicated with Frosty twice, once while he was still living and again after he passed away. Frosty's communications opened up a whole new realm for me. His words warmed my heart in a way I never dreamed possible. Communicating with animals in the physical dimension as well as a spiritual dimension sparked my scientific interest to its peak. That changed my life forever.

Pets Tell the Truth reveals my journey delving into the animal mind, plus communicating with animals, plants, and all living things and how interspecies telepathic communication has answered life's bigger questions.

Inquiry into the mind can lead to many twists and turns and even into other realms of existence. To protect my scientific reputation, stay grounded, and not delve unwittingly into the occult, I adopted a simple formula to accept my findings as valid: If I could filter my communications with animals through science, and provide a physiological or empirical basis for them, I would accept them as facts.

This book is written from the heart, but being a scientist, I also offer scientific explanations for some of the conversations and telepathic communications you are about to read. The language in *Pets Tell The Truth* is not difficult to read. This is a book for the whole family to enjoy and learn from, as we delve into the wonderful minds of our animal companions.

I invite readers to keep an open mind and take a leap of faith, and defer any judgments or opinions until they have read the animals' communications. Readers will have to leave it up to their own heart to decide whether the content and communications are true for them.

ACKNOWLEDGMENTS

I wish to thank all the persons who gave permission to tell their personal stories about their animals. I also wish to remember my sister, Florence Saracson, who helped in the typing of the manuscript, and her beautiful drawing of the Angel carrying a dog to the afterlife. Thanks to Mary Ellen "AngelScribe" and Atala Toy for their kind reviews and endorsements. Special thanks to Becky Farris for all her help understanding animals and Anna Miller who stood by me and encouraged me to pursue my dream despite chronic back pain.

The beautiful graphic design of the cover page is by Rachel Abbey of Garnett Publishing in Cleveland, Ohio, and I am delighted in her creative and artistic expression of the spiritual content of the book in this form.

Many thanks to Clyde Chafer of A Touch of Serenity Bookstore in Mentor, and Sherry Asher of Journeys Bookstore in Rocky River, Ohio, for providing space for my animal communication workshops. Thanks also to Carol Dombrose of Angel House in Strongsville for the use of her house and permission to use her dogs as animal teachers for my students.

Most of all, my deepest gratitude goes to the animals who allowed me to communicate with them and who revealed the powerful love the universe has for all life forms and the extent to which it will go for our happiness and comfort. Animal communication is a transcendental experience of its own. Touching the heart of an animal and opening up a conversation creates a beautiful bond between the animal and communicator. In this way, every animal becomes my pet as well.

This book is dedicated to Dusty and Lucky.

PART ONE
CHAPTER ONE

Frosty Introduces Me to Interspecies Telepathic Communication

"Thou hast made known unto me thy deep, mysterious things."
--The Book of Hymns, Dead Sea Scrolls

You are probably wondering how a mainstream scientist, like myself, got into interspecies telepathic communication. To the observer, empirical science with its reverence for things measurable under laboratory conditions may seem to be the extreme opposite to trans-dimensional and inter-species telepathic communication. The psychology of the mind is already difficult to measure and document and most researchers prefer to omit subjective experiences from their data altogether. It is said that necessity is the mother of invention. It is precisely that, necessity, which required me to change my way of investigating the mind, and discover a way to bridge the gap between mind and spirit. Not in my wildest dreams did I suspect that the greatest scientific discovery of my career would come from my cat. For simplification, in this and all subsequent chapters, all communications with non-human species are printed in italics.

Frosty

In late 1992, my husband Bill passed away. Just three months later, two of my nine cats contracted cancer. One cat, Missy, a brown and gray tabby, was diagnosed with terminal breast cancer. The second, Frosty, a male Seal Point Siamese, developed a brain tumor.

I took both Missy and Frosty to see a Veterinary Oncologist. Missy succumbed to her cancer and passed away. Frosty, on the other hand, had a tumor arising from the meninges, a fibrous membrane covering the brain. The tumor was putting pressure on the optic nerve assembly causing blindness. I had much experience in brain surgery on small animals and as I reviewed Frosty's x-rays and MRI along with the vet, it appeared that Frosty had a chance to recover. Although the tumor caused some of the important structures in the brain to be pushed aside, it appeared that the structures were still intact. It suggested to us that surgical removal of the tumor may be possible, removing the intracranial pressure and, in particular, that on the optic nerve assembly. The alternative was to put Frosty down. A veterinary surgical specialist agreed to do the surgery. The next day, Frosty underwent surgery and his sight was restored.

About five months later, Frosty's blindness returned. Still grieving for the loss of both Bill and Missy, the thought of another possible loss made me shudder. Frosty returned to the hospital for further tests.

The next day, the vet called me to pick up Frosty. The hospital was located about 30 to 40 minutes from my home, depending upon traffic. I arrived early, before they were officially open for business. There was a fast-food restaurant next door, so I went in to get a cup of coffee. My heart was very heavy with anxiety about Frosty. As I sat there, I quietly prayed to Saint Anthony for a miracle. Next to me on one of the tables, was a copy of the morning newspaper, the Cleveland *Plain Dealer*. I picked it up and glanced over the headlines to find something to read. I found a fascinating article about a woman in New York who could communicate with animals, even across great distances, and she was able to do this over the telephone. I tore out the article and went to pick up Frosty.

The veterinarians said they had done everything that they could for Frosty, and now it was just a matter of waiting and seeing. Later that day, Frosty's condition worsened, and as I held him in my arms, he slipped into unconsciousness. I was so frustrated, that I was beside myself. I thought about the article and the animal communicator, and decided to give it a try.

What is Telepathic Communication?

Telepathy, simply put, is long-distance feeling. It is transfer of thought from one being to another through extrasensory perception. What is being communicated is a composite of what that being sees, hears, tastes, smells, and feels at any moment. It is the total experience of the being. This composite, often called a "thought ball," is received by the telepath and then must be filtered up through the brain, decoded, and translated into language. It is not language itself. Telepathy is natural; no psychic abilities are required.

Through verbal communication with a person doing the inquiry, the telepath first makes a connection to the person, and then upon his or her request, traces the heart connection (explained below) from that person to the particular animal with whom he or she wishes to communicate. Once a connection is made, the telepath acts as an open telephone line between the two, and the person can speak directly to the animal, with the telepath acting as translator of the animal's responses to the person.

Frosty, first contact. The woman, who wanted to be called simply, "Anna," was able to communicate telepathically with Frosty for me over the phone. I asked Frosty if he knew if he was going to get well. His answer surprised and enlightened me.

"Frosty exists on a very high spiritual level," Anna said.

Frosty spoke, *I am not concerned with my physical life, only my spiritual one. I am in communication with my mate* (Missy).

Anna inquired further about his health.

My mommy is a doctor who knows everything about animals and I trust her completely.

His answer surprised me. Everyone knows that mommies know everything! The word "mommy" touched me very deeply, since Bill and I were not blessed with children. This beautiful furry creature said the words I had been longing to hear for decades, "my mommy."

Later that same day, I returned Frosty to the hospital. The veterinary staff, and especially the nurses, were very attached to him. Each took a turn holding Frosty and kissing him on his head. A few days later, they paged me at work, saying that during an ultrasound of his brain, Frosty stopped breathing. The veterinarians had intubated him (inserted a tracheal tube for ventilation), and wanted me there because they may lose him. I left work and drove directly to the hospital. I held him, and stroked his fur while the staff tried to resuscitate him. After two hours, I let him go. My final words to him were, "Thank you for everything Frosty, and we'll see each other again." Sobbing deeply, I turned over his lifeless body to the vet.

Communicating with Frosty in spirit form. If you can imagine the Grand Canyon suddenly existing inside your heart, that is how I felt after Frosty died. The death of a beloved pet is one of the worst experiences life can give you. I was inconsolable. Talking to friends, my minister, other veterinarians, and my co-workers at the hospital didn't even dent the terrible pain in my heart. My heart felt like it was in my throat, and I choked on every word spoken about Frosty. Nothing made a difference. It felt like my heart would explode like a bomb. Later in the week, sobbing, I called the animal communicator to let her know what happened, and to thank her for her assistance.

Anna said, "Oh, no! Agnes, don't cry. Frosty doesn't want that; you need to talk to Frosty."

"Is that possible?" I asked.

She assured me it was and made an appointment for that evening. I was in terrible conflict over this. I wondered if it was "forbidden" by the powers that be to talk to the dead. After much turmoil, and resigned to risk the chance of being struck by lightning for talking to spirit, I called Anna.

Anna contacted Frosty telepathically for me, and here was Frosty's communication in words as she repeated them to me: *Mommy, don't cry. I didn't go anywhere. I am still here with you. I can see you, Mommy. Can you see me?*

I answered "No."

Mommy, I am very happy here, and Daddy and Missy are with me. We are all together here. Daddy came to get me from your arms when I died. He stayed with me the whole time I was in the hospital so I wasn't scared. I am just resting now.

Oh, my goodness, it was comforting to hear Frosty say that Bill and Missy were there with him. It was the first acknowledgement that I had of Bill and Missy together in the afterlife. I asked him if he knew how much the doctors and nurses who took care of him loved him.

Mommy, I was supposed to get them to love me. It was my mission in life.

His mission? This darling little creature had a mission? His mission was to teach humans love? Animals are here to teach us love! I suddenly realized how my knowledge and appreciation of animals was only a tiny speck compared with a wealth of love and devotion given to us by animals.

Animals vary in their level of spiritual enlightenment. In some instances, animals can be so highly evolved, that it becomes a great honor to communicate with them, as if you were talking with a saint. It is nothing less than astounding what animals say about the extent the powers of the universe will go to in order to bring love to you. It is a humbling experience to communicate with animals and other life forms. The experience of inter-species telepathic communication itself is nothing less than life-transforming.

The heart connection. To understand the nature of how one is able to locate an animal to communicate with, it is necessary here to define the "heart connection." It is a band of energy which connects one being with another by an attraction and attachment to the heart. It is something that can be "seen" with clarified inner vision, that is, across the screen of your consciousness sometimes referred to as the "third eye." It looks like a distortion of air above a heat source, like a candle. As the flame warms the air surrounding it, the air expands and also rises.

As light hits the warm air, the light bends causing a distortion of anything that lies behind the candle. This heart connection is composed of a strong energy which maintains its connection with the person, pet, home, or other objects over great distances, even across continents, oceans, and even across dimensions like the afterlife.

The Pain That Wouldn't Go Away.

For three years after Frosty's death, I would find my pillow and hair all wet with tears when I awoke in the morning, but didn't know why. I didn't remember having any upsetting dreams. It really began to get to me, so I went to talk to a psychologist. He couldn't find any reason for the deeply repressed sadness. I told him about Frosty during the course of our conversations. I longed to hold Frosty's fat, hot body once more. Although the psychologist didn't believe in animal communication, or spirit for that matter, he knew me well enough to know that I was sincere in my efforts to understand. Finally, he recommended that I talk with the animal communicator again. Anna answered my call with hesitation. She said that Frosty had been dead for three years, that animals have to go into a very deep sleep, and it is really hard to connect with them on that spiritual level. Because I was crying, she did try. Anna said that Frosty was still very connected to me by a strong, inner spirit. She said to just know he is well, and that he remains in my heart's energy field.

Animals and reincarnation. About a year later, my favorite kitty, Puff, died of a heart attack in my arms. Puff was an orange long hair Maine Coon. His big, fluffy tail was something to behold indeed! Puff was the first kitty I adopted, and his disposition was so beautiful and laid back, that it made it possible for me to adopt many others. He set the tone for the whole family, including me. The night he died, I tried to call Anna, but she was out of town. Her sister, Beth, answered the call. Again, because I was sobbing, she contacted Puff.

I am outside the house by the big oak tree where the raccoons live. I am a kitten again and I can climb trees. My joints don't hurt any more, Mommy. I am free.

Through Beth, I asked him if he wanted anything, and if he was alone.

Daddy is here with me. Can't you see him?

I answered, no, delighted that Bill was there to meet him.

We can see you!

Then he said something that shook me to the core!

I think I'll be an orange kitty and come back and live with you some more.

I told Beth that he is an orange kitty. I asked if he really could come back and live with me. Beth acknowledged that he could.

Mommy, I'm going to make some noise outside tonight so you will know that I'm still here. I am going to hide in this tree and scare the raccoons when they wake up. I wonder if they're afraid of ghosts!

Our conversation ended with that. Puff's words rang in my heart. Puff wanted to come back and live with me some more! It was a dream beyond all possible dreams. I was ecstatic! I needed to confirm that possibility with Anna. That evening, I heard a commotion outside. The raccoons were scurrying down the tree, like they had seen a ghost! That rascal Puff gave me a sign that he still existed, but in another dimension and the raccoons were able to see his ghostly spirit form.

Several days later, I called Anna to confirm what Puff said about reincarnation.

"Can they do that?" I asked.

"Oh yes," she said.

She contacted Puff, to let him know I wanted him to come back. I told Puff that there was a risk. I was in my fifties, and there was a chance that he would outlive me. In that case he would have to live with my sister, Flo.

Puff paused for a minute and then said, *Well, I guess that'll be ok.*

I asked Puff if Frosty was there with him.

Don't worry about Frosty, Mommy. He is just fine.

"Invite Frosty to come back too," I said.

Frosty is still resting. He doesn't want to plan his next life yet.

Four months went by, and although I missed Puff, I was happy and content knowing he would return to me soon. It was like holding my breath for months, hoping it would really happen. I thought of him as on a sort of vacation away from me. I prayed that Anna was right. One night, I had a dream about a small orange kitten in some kind of room with a big picture window. The kitten looked at me and said, *Mommy, I'm back!* Dreams are a type of telepathic communication. They can be within the same dimension or across many different dimensions and epochs of time. I took the dream seriously and sought counsel to find him.

To confirm this I called two animal communicators, Sharon Orlando and Becky Farris, who is now my dearest friend. Through Puff, Sharon gave me details on how to find him:

I think I am about three weeks old. I am in a private home about a mile from you. Don't worry, Mommy, I have been appointed to you, so you won't miss me.

Sharon queried him further.

The house has two girls, about five and seven years old, with long blonde hair. My mother cat is black and white with orange patches, and there are six kittens beside myself, all black and white and orange patches. I am the only kitten that is all orange. My mommy cat's pregnancy was unexpected. A young girl came to visit and accidentally left the door open and she got out by mistake. I'll be ready to be picked up in three weeks. There will be an ad in the newspaper that reads: Kittens, free to good home. You will be able to get me for free. When you see me, you will recognize me right away. There will be some trouble getting me, but don't worry, you will.

Becky, without knowing my conversation with Sharon, came up with the same description from Puff about how to find him.

Three weeks came and went. I combed all the local newspapers for an ad. I called in response to one, and went to look for Puff. The ad was placed by an elderly couple who had kittens of all ages, and they were everywhere you looked. The house was full of kittens. I asked if they had two grandchildren. They didn't, and this did not match the description given to me by Becky and Sharon, so I looked further. Another ad was for a single orange kitten. The kitten turned out to be really cute, but there were no others in the litter, the mother cat wasn't black and white and orange, and besides it was a female. This was beginning to get tiresome.

One day, while at work, I picked up a copy of the *News-Herald* newspaper out of Lake County, Ohio. There was an ad that read "Kittens, free to good home." I didn't want to leave work to inquire, so I did my investigation over the phone. A lady answered my call, and I asked her if she had an orange tabby kitten. She answered yes. I asked her if the mother and six other kittens were orange, white and black. Again, she said yes. I asked her if she had two daughters with long blonde hair about five and seven years old. Again, it was yes, they were six and eight. Then I asked about the mother cat getting out of the house accidentally and if this was an unexpected pregnancy. By this time I had the poor lady going crazy.

"How do you know all this?" she asked.

I didn't want to sound too spooky, so I told her I had a dream. Then I asked for her location. It was within a mile from my home. I told the lady I would take the orange one. She said it was already promised to her cousin, but I was welcome to take a look anyway. I stuck a post-it note on my laboratory door saying "Emergency, be back later." It seemed like I flew out of there, and drove off like a crazy person to find the kitten.

When I arrived, I thought of things I might say to the owners to get them to let me have the orange kitten. The husband and girls were also home at the time. The kitten did have a look in its eyes like it knew me. I gave the couple a real sob story about how I was a widow, and I had no children, and that my own orange kitty died. I really laid it on thick. They kept apologizing, but would not give me the kitten because he was promised to their cousin. Disappointment was all over my face, and my eyes welled up with tears. They said to call back around 7:00 p.m. I left their home with terrible anxiety in my heart and went home to call Becky and Sharon, who both acknowledged that it was Puff.

Don't worry mommy, I was meant to be yours, so you won't miss me. Just keep praying.

Becky lit candles and offered up prayers to the universal powers for me. When I called back at 7:00 p.m., the woman said she talked to her uncle, and he was not going to give up the kitten. She felt very sorry for me. I started to cry and could hardly talk. Her husband got on the phone and said to call back around 9:00 p.m.

I was beside myself. My brain felt like mush. I couldn't bear the thought that my precious Puff was back, and was going to live with a stranger. I prayed for a miracle. Becky assured me that something would happen and I would get him. At 9:00 p.m. I called again. The woman answered. She said that her husband explained the situation to her cousin, who was promised the kitten. He gave him a sob story that paralleled mine, and finally the cousin said that if it means that much to her, let her have him, and he would pick another kitten. I could have him! I was mad with joy! Her husband picked up on my excitement, and warned me to drive slowly and safely, because the kitten wasn't

Dusty, Peanut & Frosty Too

going anywhere. I went to pick him up. There he was, my Puff, all ready to come home. The couple said they really wanted me to have him because they thought the kitten would complete me (a lonely widow with no kids). They were so kind, and I really appreciated their efforts. I thanked them over and over, and brought Puff home.

To protect him from the other adult cats, I put Puff in the library with his food and litter box. Becky called and she connected with Puff.

Mommy, I remember the house. I know where the litter box is. I want to come out to see the other cats. They know it's me.

I let him out. Sure enough, he went right over to play with the other cats. They thought he was the greatest thing ever. I asked each one how they felt.

Squirt said, *I think he's cute.*

Dusty said, *I'm glad you're back with us.*

Lucky said, *I think he's a brat. I don't like this adolescent age.*

Little Child, a sassy, long hair Maine Coon said, *Don't mess with me. I've had a hard life and I want to be left alone.*

Kitty said, *I'm not impressed. You don't look any different to me.*

Peanut was the last to answer, *I don't get it; how can you be big and get little?*

We explained that only the body was different, and that the same Puff spirit was what came back. He just couldn't get the concept of reincarnation, so he hissed at Puff for about a week before he would accept him. We asked Puff what he wanted his name to be.

I want to be called Puff, too! I named him Puff Too.

Frosty Returns.

Frosty's return was a little different. I had a dream that he was ready to come back. I contacted him and he said, *I'd like to be a black cat.* I warned him that sometimes people look for black cats, especially on Halloween, and they do bad things to them.

How about a black and gray striped kitty?

"Frosty, you can be whatever your little heart desires. I'm just glad that you're coming back." He said he would be back in about a month. I asked how I could find him.

I don't want to be born in a home. I want to be born in a shelter. A woman will tell you about me.

I agreed, and waited. Meanwhile, Becky and Sharon were getting mixed messages from Frosty. Sometimes we connected with an orange cat, and sometimes a black and white cat that was much younger. I started to comb all of the local animal shelters. There were so many. Becky contacted Frosty for clarification.

I will be in a shelter that has a double door at the entrance. Behind that door is the cat room. Off to the right is the dog room.

I checked out all the local shelters, and the only one that fit that description was the Lake County Humane Society. I called every day to see if kittens had come in. No luck. I also checked a local animal shelter maintained by the City of Euclid. There were kittens there, but none black and white. The woman in charge handed me a business card of a lady who rescues cats. She collects stray and feral cats, cleans them up, provides them with veterinary care, spays and neuters them and places them up for adoption at the local pet supplies stores. I called her and told her what I was looking for. She abruptly told me that I was too fussy, and that there were many kittens that needed good homes. I insisted on a black and white male.

About two weeks went by, and the Lake County Animal Shelter was having a special adoption day, and of course, I attended with my hopes high. They had so many black and white kittens I didn't know what to do. How could I possibly know which one was Frosty? Totally bewildered, I looked around the shelter and an orange adult cat caught my eye. He looked just like my old Puff, a Maine Coon with the long orange fluffy hair and tail. He had been shaved all over his body except his tail and face. His eyes were badly infected. They named him Leroy, because he was found in Leroy Township. I don't know why, but I became mysteriously drawn to him, and went over to hold him. He was a docile, relaxed, sweet kitty just like my old Puff. I wasn't particularly drawn to any of the black and white kittens there, so I left, disappointed. The next week, I went back to look at more kittens. Leroy was still there. Something drew me to Leroy again, and told me to adopt him. I couldn't help myself. I couldn't believe what I just did. I didn't need another cat, I already had seven! I just wanted Frosty back.

When I got home, I called Becky.

"You're not going to believe what I just did. I adopted another cat – not Frosty. I know that I must be crazy, but somehow I know this cat."

Becky contacted the cat.

"He knows you too," Becky said. "This is the first time he has been a cat. He knew you in his last life."

I never had any pets besides cats. I couldn't place him.

Becky said, "He was your pet, and he was with you every day. You called him by a people name."

"Bobby?" I shouted. When I said "Bobby," Becky said Leroy's face lit up like a light bulb being turned on. He was Bobby my hamster from the lab. Bobby was an experiment that didn't work, but he was so darling, I couldn't part with him, so I kept him as a pet. Every day he would share my donut with me at breakfast, and would just sit or walk around on my desk. I bought him a clear plastic ball that he could walk around in, and he would roll the ball down the hallway to visit the other labs, and they would play with him. When he died, Bill buried him in our back yard. I told Leroy that I remembered him as Bobby.

I was not meant to be with you in this incarnation. I was adopted by a young couple, who never loved me. One day they wanted to get rid of me, and threw me out of an open window of their car, down into a ravine. I think I was about 12 weeks old at the time. I was badly hurt from the fall.

I asked how he stayed alive all alone at that age in the winter.

There was a nice lady who would leave food for me on the back porch. I slept under the porch to keep warm. My eyes were burning, and my eyelids were swollen shut. A man (from the Humane Society) *came and picked me up. He brought me to the shelter where they put some creamy stuff in my eyes, and shaved off my fur to get all the burrs out of it. Your husband Bill in the spirit world contacted me and made all the arrangements for you to find me.*

This was why we were getting conflicting messages. While looking for Frosty, this animal was also sending messages to be found. Even Bill was part of this plan. I asked Bobby what he wanted his name to be.

I don't want another people name. I want to be named after Royalty.

I made a list of possible names; Prince Valiant, Prince Charles, etc. He didn't like the name Prince. I continued on the list. When I said the name Nanda, he jumped in and said, *That's the one! I am Nanda.* Nanda is the name of Krishna's father, and the word means "sweet boy child." Nanda made a good choice.

A few days after Nanda came to live with me, I really became discouraged about finding Frosty.

"Frosty, where are you?" I moaned as Becky contacted him.

I don't know where I am. I am in a box (cage) *in someone's house or store. Don't worry, Mommy, I was appointed to you, no one can touch me.* Appointed? Appointed by whom? I wondered. About 10:00 p.m., I had already gone to bed when I received a call from the cat rescue lady.

"Are you still looking for a black and white kitten? I have two, a male and female. They are in the center cage at the local pet supplies store. See if you like either of them." I answered that I wanted the male. (Remember that Frosty said a woman would tell me about him.)

I checked with Sharon and Becky to be sure it was Frosty. They confirmed my communication with him.

The next morning I went to pick him up. He had been there for a week, but no one adopted him because he had chronic diarrhea. I took him directly to my vet for treatment. He treated Frosty with Barium, to coat his intestinal lining. It helped some, but he would still have episodes of diarrhea. Finally, he gave him a drug for parasites called Flagil, and this worked. It took about three months to restore him to a healthy state, but I was so happy to have him back. I asked him what name he wanted, and he said, *You can call me Frosty if you like that name.* I told him that I loved the name, so he became Frosty Too.

Peanut enters the afterlife.

Sometime later, my eight-year-old orange tabby Peanut developed bone marrow dysplasia. He was unable to keep his red blood cell count up. The veterinary specialist tried a transfusion, but it only helped for a single day. His immune system began recognizing his red blood cells as foreign matter, and he was lysing (cutting or killing) the cells faster than he could make new ones. I was at the hospital when the vet told me that there was little else they could do. This condition came upon him so fast, I was not prepared. He was dying. My heart sank. I called Becky and spoke with Peanut.

It doesn't matter whether I get another transfusion or not, Mommy, I won't live through the night. I don't want to die alone; I want to die in your arms.

Because of his reaction to Puff's return, I explained to Peanut what was going to happen; his spirit would leave his body and go into the spirit world. He could return to me in another body, just like the others did. He still didn't get it.

I don't really understand, Mommy, but I trust you. So let me go now.

I thanked him for all that he gave me, and the vet gave him the euthanasia injection. When Peanut entered the spirit world, he was still confused. Later, during a workshop with Anna, Peanut spontaneously communicated with Anna.

You said I would leave my body, Mommy, but you didn't tell me I was going to DIE in order to do that! I understand it now. I am going to rest, and then I want to come back to you like the others.

Peanut and Dusty's pact.

Prior to Peanut's death, my cat Dusty developed diabetes. I had learned to communicate with animals myself by this time. I asked Dusty if he wanted to be put down. I explained to him that he would have to get insulin shots every day if he continued to live.

I am not finished with my MISSION yet. Yes, I do want the shots, and I want you to give them to me.

I agreed. I asked him about his mission, but he wouldn't answer. Some animals will tell you their mission: others don't want their persons to know.

Peanut returned to me within the year as a female Persian Seal Point. He said he wanted to try something completely different this time. He chose the name Misty for this life. After Misty was with us for about three months, Dusty died.

I am finished with my MISSION now.

"What was your mission, Dusty?" I asked.

Before Peanut died, we made a PACT that I would stay until he came back and got adjusted to his new body and the house. Then I would leave.

He and Peanut made a PACT? Animals make secret commitments with each other. For example, after Bill died, I sold the big house and moved into a condo. I simply couldn't afford the house any more. During this heartbreaking and stressful time, Dusty said, *Don't worry, Mommy, we talked among ourselves, and we agreed to pull back our energy fields, and lay them down in the new house. We'll make the new house as happy as this one.* They TALKED AMONG THEMSELVES? They decided what I needed, and had a plan? It was mind-boggling. Incredible! Their plan worked. It felt strange at first, but when we moved, within two days, the house "felt" the same as the other one. Dusty was right. The positive energy that permeated the big house also filled this one. The cats did this of their own accord. They did it for me. I knew then that anywhere my animals were, my heart was also. This was my true home – with my animals.

Past Lives.

Animals remember past lives. They pass from life to life as easily as we breathe, and they usually return. Each animal has a special person that they are assigned to by the universal powers that be. Animals won't tell me if they are appointed by God or by angelic beings, and it doesn't really matter. The point is that they come into a life to assist their person on his or her spiritual journey. They are a part of a person's energy; the love and spirit energy that makes each individual unique. They have always been with an individual in one form or another. They are the loyal companions of that person's soul, always offering their lives and souls for the benefit of their human. They are capable of collaborating with other non-human life forms to bring about favorable conditions to ease a person's journey in life. They can telepathically send thoughts to help a person make wise decisions.

I asked Becky's wolf, Dusty Rose, why people don't remember their past lives. She answered that humans choose not to remember because it enhances the excitement of the adventure of the life they are in now.

The thinking processes of humans are quite different from other non-human animals and plants. Although humans may excel in logical thought and intellectual pursuits, in many ways animals are higher in spiritual development than humans. Communicating with animals can be a transcendental experience in itself. Once one learns how to connect with animals, it is like entering a nice cozy warm room on a cold winter's day. One experiences the love and warmth of their world. One cannot imagine a Heaven that would be better.

The different characteristics of human thought versus animal thought are discussed in detail in Chapter Seven, *How Animals Think*.

CHAPTER TWO

Animals as Fellow Spiritual Beings in Creation

"Ask the very beasts, and they will teach you;
Ask the wild birds, and they will tell you;
Crawling creatures will instruct you;
Fish in the sea will inform you;
For which of them all knows not that this is the Eternal's way,
In whose control lies every living soul,
And the whole life of man."

— Job 12:7-10

A lovely woman named Jacquelin Smith, of Columbus, Ohio, was the first to teach me how to communicate with animals. Her course was one day, and during all of the morning session she talked about animals as fellow beings. Jacquelin had a very gentle manner about her, and I could easily appreciate that she was totally connected with beings of all kinds. I don't know if it was what she said, or if it was the impression of completeness that radiated from her, but by the end of the morning, the students in her class, me included, were convinced that there was an essence in all life that she was able to recognize. We wanted to learn how to perceive that essence too.

Jacquelin spoke about treating animals as fellow beings, just as we would people. For example, she told us to ask permission before we reach to touch an animal.

"Think how you would feel if a total stranger came up to you and touched you?" she said. These are all simple courtesies that we extend to anyone we meet. The same is true when contacting an animal telepathically. You must first say, "Hello," and then "May I speak with you?" Jacquelin explained it is also good practice to talk to your pets as you come and go during the day. If there are other humans living in your home, wouldn't you extend them the courtesy of letting them know where you are going and what time you will return? Extend animals that same courtesy; they worry about you when you are not there.

During the afternoon, Jaquelin's workshop participants had the chance to communicate with an animal. The teaching animal was a Shelty who belonged to one of the participants. Jacquelin asked each of us to ask the dog a simple question that his person could validate. She taught us how to enter a quiet meditative state to connect with the animal. I asked, "What is your favorite treat?"

As a response, the dog sent me two pictures (which I saw flash across the screen of my consciousness): a dog biscuit and then a beef jerky. When it came my turn, I told the group of my communication. The woman who owned the dog said, "Oh, no, he's a vegetarian – he never eats meat." Just then, another student, who turned out to be her daughter, said, "Oh, yes he does. I give him beef jerky as a treat when he comes to our house." The dog was telling two truths, one favorite treat came from the older woman and the other treat came from her daughter.

The animal spirit form.

For our second communication with the Shelty, the instructions were to ask something more difficult. I had very little experience with dogs: as a child, we always had cats as pets (mouse catchers, actually). My only experiences were with neighbors' dogs, and I was afraid of them. One neighbor owned a pit-bull terrier that without provocation would bite my legs every day as I walked to kindergarten. Each day, when I got to school, the nurse had to clean and dress my wounds. She called my parents, who blamed me for provoking the dog. Of course, I didn't. One day, my father quietly followed me to school and caught the dog in the act. He grabbed the dog and went rounds with its owners and that ended that! A second dog, a poodle, would always hump my legs. I related this to the Shelty. I said, "I am afraid of dogs because I have no experience with them, but I want to help dogs that are sick or in pain. What can I do?"

Just get to know us better.

"How?"

I'll show you.

Just then, he sent me a picture or image of his spirit form. It was a beautiful ball of white light approximately the same size as his body, but floating above the ground about 18 inches. The white light energy body looked like the nucleus of an atom, with the energy of thousands of electrons swirling around and through it in every direction. It looked similar to close-up pictures I had seen of the sun's surface. The ball of light sent out to me a loving energy that seemed to surround my entire body. At that moment a revelation came over me. I immediately recognized the energy ball as the same spirit, which also existed in me, and in ALL LIFE. No words could have described the experience of unity consciousness of that moment, with complete universal understanding of all dogs everywhere. The Shelty then walked over to me and laid down by my legs and feet and began to playfully roll himself over on them. I moved to the floor so I could hold and cuddle him. The experience was of complete love and understanding - a sense of wholeness, as if we were one being. I knew then what the beautiful glow I saw earlier in Jacquelin was coming from. She was able to connect and become one with that unity consciousness.

Validating communications.

After the introductory workshop with Jacquelin, I practiced telepathic communication with pets belonging to friends. I went about it like it was a research project. I wrote an entire protocol of questions to ask every animal so I could compare answers both among species and within species. I also wanted to be sure to validate my communications with the owners. To test my skill, I would call a friend and ask permission to speak with his or her dog, cat or bird. Most of my communications came to me visually, so I would ask the pet to show me where they were at the moment. Then, I would validate their answers with their owners over the phone. If Kitty showed me she was sleeping on the floor of the closet next to her owner's brown high heels, I would tell the friend, and she would confirm it for me. I gave details of the image being received, including the distance between the cat and the shoes, what clothes were hanging just over the cat, etc. Then I asked animals to do things like look out the window and show me what they were seeing. If the animal sent an image of a group of kids playing baseball in the street, I would write down the details of number of kids playing, how many boys versus girls, an estimate of how old they were, what they were wearing, and so on. Since many of these animals lived close by, I would then drive to their house to determine for myself how accurate the images were to the actual street scene. Then I would check over my notes, checking off each detail. I was astonished at how accurate the images were that the animals telepathically sent me. I did this over and over, to rule out that I was creating the image myself. Jacquelin told me that the animal sends an overall impression of what the animal is seeing, hearing, feeling, tasting, sensing, and thinking all at the same time. This impression, or "thought ball" as it is called by some investigators, is received, filtered up through the brain, decoded, translated and converted to language by the receiver. It is not language itself. This is based largely upon knowledge existing in a person's mind. For example, if one person asked an animal how he was feeling, he or she would get something like, "I have an upset tummy." If I asked the same animal, because of my medical training, it would show me a 3-dimensional x-ray image of its alimentary tract, and the location of the discomfort — whether it existed in the stomach, intestines, or whatever — and details of the physiology of the discomfort (like gastric motility, etc.). Thus, there are individual differences not only among animals, but also among animal communicators. In Chapter Nine, I will explain more about how telepathy works.

CHAPTER THREE

Farm Animals

After I was satisfied that I was receiving valid communications, I enrolled in Anna's advanced workshop at her farm in Rochester, New York. I was among 13 participants in the class, and was surprised to find out that three of us were neuroscientists. Abby, a woman from Illinois, and I shared the bunk room and became good friends. The farm had about 50 different animals: horses, ponies, chickens, donkeys, llamas, and ducks. All were good communicators. We practiced each day with as many as we could. Anna would confirm our communications. Being scientists, Abby and I were concerned that Anna was the only one giving validations. One evening, we agreed to practice with each other. I had photographs of all my cats, and demonstrated to Abby the way I was taught to communicate. Abby practiced with my animals. She was right on target with her communications with them, describing in detail the interior of my home, and even that there were two large trees down in the ravine. My cats had never been outdoors, so I didn't understand how she could get that answer. I queried one of my cats.

We know the trees are in the ravine, because the raccoons that come to our patio door showed us where they hide until dark so they can get the bread you leave for them.

So, animal-to-animal communication appeared to work the same way as human-to-animal communication.

Spiritual blessings from animals. Next, it was my turn to practice communicating with Abby's animals. She wanted me to talk to her donkey, Chester. I contacted Chester and asked him to show me the yard and house so Abby could validate my communications. He started showing me his fenced area — to the left was the barn and to the right was the house. The house was a white frame ranch with a red shingle roof. The front door, also red, was off to the right and had an aluminum screen door, and two windows on the right. Chester was standing in front of a large oak tree, so I couldn't see the left half of the house. I communicated this to him.

Oh! I'm sorry, I'll move over so the tree is not in the way. Can you see the rest of the house now?

Once he moved, I could see the rest of the house in detail. I saw two picture windows, a large one to the left and a smaller one toward the middle. Chester was not by himself; there were three girls in uniforms (like the 4-H Club or Girl Scouts) standing in front of him. Two looked about seven or eight years old, and a taller girl with brown braids looked about twelve. Abby immediately responded, "These are children in my Girl Scout troops."

When I thanked Chester for his communication with me, something very beautiful occurred. Chester said, *Bless you for helping my mommy.* When the word "bless" came out of his mouth, along with it came a ball of pure white light energy like the one I experienced with the Shelty. This ball of light energy traveled across space and time from Illinois and it entered the kitchen in New York where we were sitting. As it entered the kitchen, it became visible to the screen of my consciousness, and appeared to come from the upper corner of the wall, hit me in the chest and went directly into my heart. As it impacted me, I felt waves of love and gratitude rippling over my whole body. A tremendous loving sensation filled my chest that was very powerful, but very gentle. It occurred to me that when someone sends a blessing, it is not just a metaphor, but an actual transfer of spiritual energy from one being to another.

After that, Abby wanted to try. I told her that one of my cats, Frosty, was a very old soul, and that she could ask him anything. She asked him to show her God. The image he sent her was a very bright white light with rays shooting out in every direction like a sunburst.

Animal communication turned out to be so much more than either of us had ever imagined. This was not about asking Fido not to poop on the neighbor's lawn, or Kitty to stop clawing the furniture. Abby and I realized that it was an entry into a higher state of consciousness or dimension where something of the divine could be experienced.

As the week went on, I took the opportunity to communicate with a donkey named Buddy in the barn. After my communication with Abby's donkey Chester, I really wanted to get to know a little more about how donkeys think. I introduced myself.

"Hello, my name is Agnes, may I speak with you?"

You'll like me. I'm really smart!

"Oh, how is that?"

I can hear real good. I watch over the farm and when I hear danger approaching, I let out this sound (hee —haw). *I'm like their burglar alarm!*

"Is it okay if I touch you? I have never petted a donkey before"

Sure. Touch me all you like.

"Tell me, Buddy, how do you hear so well and act as an alarm?"

Buddy sent me a telepathic impression that fascinated me. He sent what he hears and where it is located. First, he sent an auditory impression that seemed far away, and I spontaneously "knew" that it was sounds coming from about a mile away. It was a very clear audio signal and the sounds of the farm and inside the barn were totally absent. To illustrate, the sounds were like those you receive when listening through an open window on the fifth story of a building, except it came from all directions, as if you are on the top of a Ferris wheel. You hear clearly the sounds of boats, trains, and church bells in the distance, but cannot discern sounds coming from people talking on the ground below you. I could clearly hear wild animals walking about on the surrounding countryside, the sound of the Amtrak train as it moved along, and the crickets in the distance, but nothing close by. Next, Buddy sent me the sounds surrounding the farm outside the barn. Again, the sounds inside the barn were totally absent. Then he sent me what he hears inside the barn. I could hear the sounds of the barn animals, and also clearly pick up the footfalls of a mouse nearby. I asked Buddy how this was done.

I have the ability to focus my audio reception to varying distances at will, and to omit the ones I don't want to listen to.

How is this possible?

It's these big ears; they turn to detect certain sounds at different distances. It's the way I listen for predators that may harm me or the other animals here.

"Is it the shape of your ears, Buddy?"

Yes, the tallness of my ears can be pointed in any direction as an amplifier. If I move them slightly, and open them widely, the sounds closer by are picked up.

I thanked Buddy for the explanations of his remarkable tele-audio abilities.

Two orange cats at the farm really stole my heart. Both males, one was 21 years old (the father cat) and the other 20 years old (the son). The father cat was probably the happiest animal I have spoken to yet. They lived with an elderly couple until the woman died, and the husband went into a nursing home.

I had a wonderful life! My persons loved me, treated me well, and made me happy. Now, I am looking back on all the wonderful years we had together.

The other orange cat, the son, came over and sat down next to me.

"Hello," I said.

Hello, I see you are talking to my dad. We lived with this couple and the lady died.

"Yes, that's what your father told me. You two seem to get along very well."

Yes, we have enough love to share with each other and everyone.

How I wished I could adopt these two. Just then, the father cat sent me a question.

Do you have a husband?

"No, my husband died."

Maybe you can marry our dad and we can all live together again.

That really tickled my heart. These two adorable cats were trying to find a way to have me marry their person so I could be their mommy and they would have their daddy back. Too precious for words!

Communicating with plants.

During the workshop, I was having difficulties with my back and had to lay on the floor for relief a good deal of the time. As the workshop came to a close, Anna asked us to pick a tree, plant, or rock to communicate with. We were instructed to ask "What do you have to teach me today?" I walked outside, looking around the grounds for something to catch my eye. Near the driveway entrance stood two statues of cats with angel wings. I knew this place had my name written all over it. I looked at a plant growing between the statues, with soft, broad leaves almost like a pumpkin or melon leaf. Some leaves had brown spots on them. There was no fragrance. (Later I found out it was a hollyhock.) I telepathically connected with the plant.

"Hello," I said, and introduced myself.

I love the wind, moving my branches (arms and legs) *about. It feels like I am floating. My roots are very secure in the ground, so I can bounce and float with whatever is happening.* Just then, a brisk breeze came by. *Whee-e, this is fun. I am bouncing up and down. Sometimes rain hits me and gives me a bath that is cool and refreshing. Sometimes ants crawl up me and tickle me* (giggles).

The plant had a very child-like personality, which gave utterances that were half giggle and half scream, like a toddler about eighteen months old being swung by its arms in a circle or under a person's legs. There was a dandelion near it, touching its leaves.

"What is this?"

It's a sunshine flower (giggles).

The way she said it, it sounded like "lollipop."

"What are these spots on your leaves here?"

Freckles.

"Do you have a name?"

Ermine. My name is Ermine. I lived here a long time ago, in another lifetime when I was a human baby.

"You were a human baby? Can humans become plants?"

You can become anything you want. Anything is possible. I wanted to have a carefree life in which I didn't have anything to do but bounce along on the wind, and feel the rain and sunshine on my leaves.

"What message do you have for me today?"

Take life as it comes. Live joyously in the moment.

Our conversation continued and I asked her where she lived when she was a human baby, in the red house?

No, the red house wasn't here then. My family had a log cabin.

The red house was about 100 years old, so it must have been prior to the 20th century.

"What is important to you?"

Freedom. She giggled, and sent me an image of a red bouncing ball, about the size of the one in the game "jacks." I didn't understand the significance of the bouncing ball.

"What about responsibility?"

That is my responsibility!!

I asked for clarification.

I am to teach you today how to go from life experience to life experience. Just like a bouncing ball, every time you hit bottom, you just bounce (pauses) *back up!!*

Ermine sounded like a child doing somersaults. She had picked up on my health problems and my depression over them.

"Now ask me a question." No answer. "Come on, I'd consider it an honor."

You're too serious.

A few moments later, Ermine decided to send me an image of a rocking horse.

You were born to be a horse person. You should be that way again.

"I can't be a horse person with my back and neck."

Look more carefully.

I suddenly recognized the horse in the image as the rocking horse my older brother, Steve, made for me in wood shop at school when I was three years old. Gosh, I hadn't thought about that horse for almost fifty years! I spent most of my waking hours on it. I was in pure bliss.

Don't think like a doctor, but like a rider – remember the experience of being a rider!

I didn't quite understand what she meant. Later that day, when Anna asked us about our communications, she contacted Ermine telepathically, who elaborated further on the horse person. Ermine meant a centaur. Yes, of course! The sign of the centaur, half man and half horse. Now I understood. Ermine was illustrating in her toddler way, that I should remember a time when I was able to join with the horse as one being.

CHAPTER FOUR

The Procedure: How to Communicate with Animals

I discovered that everyone has the ability to communicate with animals. The human brain already has the wiring to receive telepathic communications. We were born with this ability, because humans are also members of the animal kingdom. We simply have forgotten how to use it. Telepathy is the ancient language of the peoples of the Earth. J. Allen Boone[1], the first person to write about animal communication states, "Life to the ancients was an all-inclusive kinship in which nothing was meaningless, nothing unimportant, and from which nothing could be excluded. In those days, beings made no separating barriers between animal, vegetable, mineral, and man. The whole Earth was of one language and speech. At one time, every living thing was in rational correspondence with everything else, and all life was in full accord."

Telepathy is the universal language, just, as some believe, is music and rhythmic drumming. It has always been a mystery how African drumming communicated language to neighboring tribes. Linguists who study such things found that drumming lacked a sufficient number of sounds or beats to be decoded into any discernible language. As it turns out, the drumming was merely a signal to the tribe to be quiet and listen for incoming telepathic messages. It is like your telephone ringing to indicate someone is trying to communicate with you. The drumming alerted the people and put them into a spontaneous altered (quiet, listening) state. The telepathic messages were then exchanged. These skills can be restored by knowing a little bit about how they work.

The most important factor in learning to communicate is to remove any blocks about viewing animals as fellow beings. When properly humble, it happens very easily. When you appreciate an animal's spiritual qualities, you will soon recognize that they are also qualities of your own soul. This mutual understanding of the sacredness of all life opens the door to communication.

A second factor is simply learning to listen. This requires a quiet mind; that is, meditative states in which random thoughts are gently pushed aside. Sometimes it is useful to think of the being you wish to communicate with as someone from outer space, someone about whom you have no preconceived notions. Because you do not know their culture, you make no judgments about what you will hear or learn. What I am trying to illustrate by this example is to be completely open and non-judgmental. Don't edit what you hear in any way. Just listen.

In the following paragraphs I will present a meditation that I find useful to guide one into an altered state. When you connect with an animal, you are not connecting with the brain. You are connecting with the animal's spirit. I have done much research on this topic. The telepath cannot be connecting with the brain. Otherwise, how can one communicate with a disembodied spirit that has no brain? It is as easy to connect with an animal on the "other side" as it is to connect with an animal in a physical body. Trust me on this for now, and I will explain more in later chapters.

The procedure.

The first thing to learn and experience is what it feels like to have a quiet mind, and what it is to be in an altered state of awareness. The altered state is not a trance like mediums use: it is simply a meditative state in which random thoughts are gently eliminated. Once you learn to quiet your mind and experience what it feels like to receive a message, you will be able to do it automatically: it will become like an everyday occurrence.

1. You will need a small vase or similar object. The purpose of this exercise is to train your mind to hold that image, so that you can examine it carefully. First, look at the object with your eyes open, then close your eyes and continue to see the object with your eyes closed. Now open your eyes and continue

to see that object with your inner eye, across the screen of your consciousness. Look away from the physical object, and continue to see the object. Telepathy resides in the realm of imagination. The word "telepathy" comes from the Greek word "imago" meaning to create a duplicate or likeness in the mind. When you look at the object, and then look away, continue to see the object. It is no different than remembering what a piece of apple pie looks like even though it is no longer there. You are seeing the object with your inner eye, third eye, or inner vision. Now look at the vase or object and then move the object with your mind so it is in the corner of the room. Make the object move anywhere in the room you want.

2. Next, begin communicating with an animal by using a photograph of an animal that you don't know. The purpose of this exercise is to communicate without being confused by the body language of the animal or by preconceived notions of the animal's answers. It is helpful to use photographs of a neighbor or friend's pet. After you receive an answer, let the friend tell you if you are correct. By your friend validating the answer, your confidence in your ability will rise quickly. Before you speak with the animal, ask permission. It is necessary to ask permission of the spirit to communicate with it. When listening, just accept the answer without judgment, just as if you were listening to a space alien. When you are finished, say thank you. Afford the animal the same courtesy that you would when speaking to a human. Remember you are speaking to a sentient being. Honor it as

being of the same spiritual essence as all life including your own.

3. The meditation: Sit comfortably in a chair. Take a few deep breaths, in and out. Place both feet so they are flat on the ground. Close your eyes. Feel your feet connecting with the ground, and imagine that there are roots, coming out of the bottom of your feet, growing deep into the rich soil. They go deep into the earth and you feel secure and grounded. Now imagine that your body is like the trunk of the tree, standing strong, tall, and secure. Next, imagine that your arms and head are the branches of the tree, reaching out to the universe to take in all its energy, wisdom, and love. Now imagine that you see the branches of the tree begin to separate in the middle. A scene that was hidden between the branches begins to all open up. This scene is that of a lake, very beautiful and very still. Around the lake there are beautiful trees and plants. As you look at the lake, you notice that there is no wind or breath of air. The trees are motionless, and the water in the lake lies perfectly still, just like a sheet of glass. Continue to look at the stillness of the lake. All is peaceful and quiet. On the opposite side of the lake of where you are standing, you begin to notice a small bridge that crosses a stream. You and the lake are on one side of the stream: an animal stands on the other side. It is the animal you want to communicate with. Send him a telepathic message, such as, "Hello." Ask for permission to speak. Say, "May I speak with you?" When you hear the animal answer "Yes," begin your conversation. When you are finished say, "Thank you, and

now I release you and you can release me."

4. During your conversation, do not cross over the bridge in the meditation scene. Stay grounded in the physical dimension on your side of the stream. Do not let the animal cross over to your side either. If you cross the stream, you will still communicate, but you will not remember it when you come out of the meditation. You need your physical brain to decode and translate the communication and store it in memory for you to recall it. Always stay grounded in the physical dimension while you are communicating in the telepathic dimension.

5. Take a few moments to assimilate what you have received. Practice this technique with different photos until you know what it feels like to receive an incoming message. Then practice with the living animals. It is best to practice with a neighbor or friend's animal for the same reasons. Once you are confident, you can speak to your own animals. The most important thing to remember is to not judge or edit what you get.

Some people are unable to "visualize" the animal as described above. Among my students, I have discovered that many men are unable to visualize even simple objects like an ice cream cone. For women, sometimes intuition comes to them not through the "third eye," but through the heart chakra. It is more like a feeling of warmth and then a sudden "knowing." If the exercise above does not work for you, then try opening your heart accepting whatever comes to mind. Let the impression enter your heart as an experience. The "knowing" will come with it.

The most frequent question I am asked when teaching others

to communicate with animals is, how do you know the response is coming from the animal or not just your imagination trying to figure out an answer?

Three things distinguish an animal's response: the speed of the answer, the simplicity of the answer, and the absence of dualities and value judgments (Chapter Seven). An animal's answer to a telepathic question will most likely be sent and the answer received, before the question is even out of your mouth. By this I mean that during communications, I usually speak in words so the person can hear what I am saying to their pet. Sometimes, I just communicate mentally. The telepathic connection is not from one brain to another, but from one spirit energy field to another. Animals have very simple answers because they do not have to filter the content through the ego's restrictions as humans do. Animals do not experience dualities, because that would require a value judgment, which animals do not do.

In summary of the differences described above, if an answer implies unity, connectedness, benevolence, and is non-judgmental, it is from the animal. If the answer implies separateness, dualities, polarities, or evaluations and judgments, it is from you.

The Protocol.

All communications with animals, plants, trees, rocks and other life forms other than clients' animals received the same protocol or questionnaire so I could compare individual differences and species.

1. Are you comfortable communicating with me?
2. May I ask you some questions?
3. Can you show me where you are right now?
4. What is it like to be a dog, etc.?
5. How do you view humans?
6. Can you communicate with others in your species?
7. Can you communicate with other species?

8. What makes you happy?

9. What makes you unhappy?

10. Do you dream? What do you dream?

11. Do you remember a past life? What were you in that lifetime?

12. Do you have a mission? What is your mission?

13. How did you come to be in this particular home, zoo, etc?

14. Who are your friends?

15. Do you communicate telepathically with other animals?

16. Do you form groups of friends?

17. What do you like to do? What activity?

18. Do you like your food? What is your favorite?

19. What is your perception of children? And of adults?

20. What is your perception of God?

21. What do you see as errors that humans make?

22. When you were born, did you have a choice of species? Of color of fur? Of gender?

23. Who grants these choices? Did you pick your animal mother?

24. Who determines where you will be born or who will be your person?

25. Were you ever a human? A plant? A rock?

26. Does your species have a special mission in evolution?

27. What do you do when you are ill and no human notices? How do you heal yourself?

28. What emotions do you have, e.g. sadness, guilt, joy, happiness, hope, etc.?

29. If you could have anything you wanted, what would make you the happiest?

30. Is there something you would like all humans to know?

CHAPTER FIVE

Wild Animals

Dances with Wolves.

A few months later, Becky invited me to visit her in New Mexico. A few years before, when I was just beginning to learn animal communication, she sent me Polaroid pictures of all her animals (about twenty-five in all) to practice with. All her animals are great communicators, and she uses them when teaching others. Rebecca Richerson Farris (her full name) is a veterinary technician and a professional dog trainer and operates her business under the name "Dutiful Doggies." Becky, a delightful woman with side-splitting wit, has been an animal communicator all of her life, and has used her skills with police departments to find lost or kidnapped children as well. We first became friends when Frosty was dying. Since then, we talked to each other over the phone daily, but had never met in person. I was very grateful to Becky for all her insights and sharing of knowledge about interspecies telepathic communication while I was learning. I accepted her invitation and decided to visit with her for a week. Becky said she would teach me how to talk to groups of animals, and also how she teaches dog training.

Days before I flew to Albuquerque, we realized that we didn't know what each other looked like, since we never exchanged photographs of ourselves. Becky was to pick me up at the airport. I told her I would be wearing a bright orange jacket, so she couldn't miss me when I arrived. I asked her what clothes I should bring.

"Just bring jeans and shirts — this is the wild, wild west." In Cleveland, going to dinner in the evening, one customarily dresses up, even if it is just to put on nice slacks. "You'll be the only one wearing them," she said. I never thought about where the wild, wild west was, other than in the John Wayne or Clint Eastwood movies. I didn't know what to expect. She was right! There were cowboys, Native Americans and Mexicans living in adobe homes, and people on horseback everywhere. Everyone wore jeans. It was definitely a new experience!

Becky picked me up at the airport, and we started the two-hour drive to Los Alamos. She told me she brought Raven, a wolf puppy, along with her and I would meet her in the truck. This "puppy" weighed about 75 pounds, and was not exactly the little teddy bear size I had envisioned. As we started the trip home, Raven, riding behind the front seats was very well behaved, only placing a front paw on me from time to time, and then sleeping most of the way home. Becky needed to pick up something from Wal-Mart, so she stopped the truck and said, "Be right back." When the door closed, Raven woke up and decided to climb over in front and park her butt on my lap. I sat there quietly about four inches away from those big, white, sharp teeth. I wondered if I was going to be Raven's lunch. I thought I would try what I did with the Shelty, and communicate to Raven, that I had never met a wolf before and I was a little nervous. She turned her head and opened her jaws wide. (Talk about a near-death experience!) Instead of looking through a tunnel, and seeing a white light, I was looking down a throat with large, white man-eating teeth. Raven then began licking my face as I repeated, "Nice wolf, nice wolf, pretty girl, pretty girl," which didn't calm me a bit. I let out a sigh of relief when Becky returned after a few minutes.

New Mexico is breathtaking with its rust-colored mountains. The plains look very familiar, as they are often used for western movies. Becky's wolves are trained actors who are frequently used by movie producers to film a shoot. Dusty, her oldest wolf, played opposite Kevin Costner in the movie, *Dances With Wolves*. Dusty passed away several years before. I was fortunate enough to have the opportunity to communicate with her before she died. Dusty was a beautiful, enlightened being with great wisdom. She was the first wolf Becky adopted, and because of Dusty's gentle manner, Becky adopted other wolves and became a wolf-rescue person, training them to be household pets and placing them in good homes. She had five wolves at home that I was anxious (i.e., filled with anxiety) to meet.

Becky's home is a beautiful ranch tastefully decorated in Southwestern style. All of her dogs, cats, and birds were eager to meet me because I had previously and frequently communicated with them via long distance. They refer to me as "Aunt Agnes." This time with them would allow me the opportunity to use my protocol and compare the personality and communications of several animals within the same breed and raised by the same owner.

There were many individual differences in personality, temperament, intelligence and spiritual growth among her cocker spaniels. Among them, Patches is the friendliest, and also the most spiritually evolved. She promptly took possession of my lap for the entire visit. I loved her fat, hot body as she sat on me. Patches proceeded to describe all the toys the dogs have to play with. Shadow, a black cocker, wanted to continuously play "fetch" with a tennis ball. Finally, Becky told her "Tennie go night-night." Shadow was the captain of the entertainment committee. Snap took a little while to size me up, but is friendly and I think the most intelligent. Snap has a kind of subtle, reserved, cautious, and academic persona, and if human, would surely be a systems analyst. Rusty, a rescue who Becky kept for a shelter during her heartworm treatments, was constantly at my side. Rusty acted more like a social scientist, watching the group dynamics with objective non-interference. All the cocker spaniels are good communicators, but Patches always started the conversations and kept them going. Each dog has its own favorite friend, largely based upon the compatibility of the personalities, just like humans.

The cats are also compatible, and varied in their spiritual development. Spooky was the most evolved, but is passive compared with Panda Bear. Spooky was certainly under the opinion that she was "boss" of the house. Panda said he would sleep in my bed with me because he knew that I was lonely for my own cats. Smokey, a gray Yorkie-Poo fit somewhere in between the dog and cat family, and didn't really care either, as long as someone picked her up over their head and snuggled her at least once a day.

Panda was right. I was lonely for my own cats. I had difficulty communicating with my own pets, but not others. Becky explained that talking to your own pets is more difficult, because you have your own emotional investment in them and that clouds your thinking. If one of your own animals is sick, in particular, you don't really want to hear the animal's answer to questions like, "Do you want to be put down, or released from your body?" She showed me how to overcome such blocks. "If Dusty is sick and wants to be put down, wouldn't you want to know that so he doesn't have to continue in pain?" she asked. After I thought about it, I realized she was right. It was my own emotional investment in the cats that was at risk when I communicated with them. The cats had no problem answering my questions; I am the one who blocked hearing their answers. This is true for all animal communicators. It seems hardest to communicate with our own animals. So, in the event something important is happening with one of our own pets, we tend to call another animal communicator for validation and a second opinion.

I had previously asked Becky's pets to show me what their house looked like, what their favorite treat was, where their food bowls are kept, where they slept, and so on. Although Becky validated their answers for me over the phone, I didn't realize until I arrived how accurate the perceptions and images her animals sent to me telepathically really were. When I met Becky's husband, Rob, honestly, I could have picked him out of a crowd of a thousand. Patches sent his image to me so perfectly, right down to the color of his blond hair and even the strands of hair that were highlighted from the sun.

Becky had five birds at the time, which woke up in the morning singing a certain tune. After a while it got monotonous so Becky would shout, "Change your tune," and the birds would start singing another tune. It was hilarious! Only another animal communicator can appreciate what happened. No one else would even believe us. I was introduced to the rabbits. They were in special summer cages outside. Here again, some were very enlightened beings and others were very base — interested in eating, sleeping, and getting special treats.

The wolves are the most challenging and interesting. Shalako is the most enlightened and acts as the over soul of the entire family, including dogs, cats, rabbits and wolves. Shalako claims to have some sheepherder in her, which gives her the managerial skills to keep everyone together on the same wavelength, so to speak. She acts as a counselor of sorts, guiding and reprimanding each animal as necessary to keep the peace. Shalako is also an actor, and I asked her what she dreamed.

I'd like to be in a race with wolves or dogs, a real race or even a pretend one like in the movies. I can run real fast, and I am very agile. I can outrun any dog or wolf. I like it when we make movies along a hillside or

Zorro and Shalako

canyon. Sometimes I run real fast and they (the camera men) *can't keep up with me.*

Unlike the other wolves, I felt very close to Shalako, and very comfortable in her presence.

"Your fur is absolutely gorgeous! Is it OK if I pet you?"

Yes, you may. I am very secure within myself, so I do not mind others touching me or petting me. Sometimes children even ride on me.

Shalako felt soft and warm; she let me touch her all over her body, and even turned around for me to pet the other side. It made me feel very comfortable to be with her and the other wolves.

To my surprise, when I had previously spoken to the other wolves — Puma, Raven, Yoda, Brandy, and Zorro — what I sensed was their sweetness, even more than the cocker spaniels. Zorro was the Alpha of the pack, the leader, while he was perfectly happy to have Shalako as the oversoul. I asked Shalako why this was so.

Zorro is stronger and more alert than I, and is far more capable of being the Alpha wolf than I. He is concerned with the safety and protection of the pack, while I am more concerned with the spiritual aspects of it. The pack operates as a unit, with me as the spirit, and Zorro as the body. Zorro is like a leader. He commands respect and submission from the others.

"I like the images of the house and yard you sent me Zorro," I said, trying to start a conversation.

I like the pictures you sent me of your house too.

"What pictures?"

When you communicate with us, it works two ways. I can see you, your cats, the house, and even the black squirrel that sits on the railing of the patio.

It never occurred to me that the animals were receiving images from me at the same time I was receiving them from the animals. I guessed it was like seeing a two-way TV with cameras and projectors on each side.

I go with Mommy in the car everywhere she goes. I am always with her.

Becky validated that he was telling it right.

Group Mind.

I didn't understand what Shalako meant by being the oversoul of the pack, so I asked Becky.

"This is what you are here to learn," she said. "When you talk to groups of animals, like herds, flocks, packs, schools or other groups, you can't talk to just one of them because they won't answer you. You have to talk to the whole group and the oversoul of the group will answer you.

I didn't understand.

"Think of it as if there was a large NET covering the whole group. They operate as a group mind, with each section of the net touching every other section in constant communication.

They are communicating with the others telepathically. This is how birds are able to fly in formation, moving about in unison or herds of sheep or cattle are able to stay together without individual members straying and getting lost." I always thought it was because they followed some sort of scent, or maybe a radar signal like bats, so I queried further.

"Consider schools of fish," Becky said. "What scent would they pick up to keep them in unison, even salmon, jumping in and out of the water as they attempt to return to their breeding grounds? It is by telepathy."

The next day, I had an opportunity to test her theory.

Rob offered to take us for a drive along the mountains to a place called Valle Grande. Thousands of years ago, this was the base of the volcanic eruption that formed the Jemez Mountains, a part of the Rocky Mountains. Now, it is a beautiful valley, rich in green grass and with mighty evergreens. Rob spotted a herd of elk in the valley, near the tall evergreens, so we stopped the truck and got out to enjoy them.

Becky said, "This valley is going to change soon. It is going to be made into a wildlife preserve. Construction is also planned for cabins and buildings for the Forestry Service. Ask the elk if they are aware of this and what they plan to do about it."

I telepathically connected with the herd, imagining that they had a big white fishing net over all of their heads. I waited for their answer.

Thank you for your concern. We are aware of what changes will be made. We have been aware all along, because we are in communication with all life, including humans. We have loved this valley, but understand what the Forestry Service is trying to do. We have selected several other spots in the mountains where we can go when the construction begins. We are not afraid of moving. We are in contact with the rams that live higher on the mountain and they have agreed to open their space and let us in.

"What do you mean, when you say you are connected with all life?"

Just like the net that you imagined covering our herd when you contacted us, there is a net or web-like structure that connects all life on this planet.

"Can you tell me more about this net?"

The oversoul telepathically sent me an image of a 3-dimensional net which connected everything on the Earth, including plants, trees, mountains, and all kinds of animals - human and non-human. Each intersect of the net's filament upon filament represented a life form.

Do you understand now?

"I can see it in the image you sent me, but what does it mean?"

Humans believe themselves to be separate beings in creation, so all they see is what they can see (perceive or take in) *with their five senses. Animals know they are not separate, but different expressions of the one being – the Creator of All. We can see things from many different perspectives, across great distances in an instant.*

"Is it possible for humans to see this web?"

Of course! Humans only see what they want to see (perceive or take in), *not what's really there. All you need to do is acknowledge that everything in creation is a living being, and then your mind will be open to new things, and you will be able to see how we are all connected.*

I thanked the oversoul elk for his incredible communication with me. Once the communication was over, the herd started to move off into the wooded area.

"How did you get them to give you such an in depth answer?" Becky asked.

"I don't really know. I guess the animal must have picked up on my interest in the physiology of the net and was willing to explain how it worked."

We stopped the truck again to talk to a flock of wild birds. I did the same thing as before; I talked to the group about their life in the forest and waited for an answer.

We are surprised and pleased that you are asking us about our life. No human ever talks to us.

"Do you always live here in this spot?"

No, of course we don't. We fly south for the winter.

"I thought this is the south" (New Mexico).

It is, but it gets very cold here, and there is much snow. It is too hard to stay warm, and difficult to find enough food, so we fly south until we reach a warmer climate.

"How do you know where to fly?"

We communicate with other flocks in more southern areas. If they are doing fine, then they relate to us the direction and distance to fly so we can go there too.

"How do you know where to look for a flock to communicate with them if you can't see them?"

There are always birds that act as scouts, and they are in communication with the bigger flock. They come by as messengers or news-carriers, and spread the information to others.

What sensible organizational skills, I thought. I thanked them for their communications as they flew away.

Group communication turned out to be quite different than individual pet communication. A few years later, I had the opportunity to appear on a radio show called "Angel Waves" broadcast out of Cincinnati, Ohio, with Maureen McCullough and Mary Ellen AngelScribe. Mary Ellen is the author of two books, *Expect Miracles* and *A Christmas Filled With Miracles*. She was a gracious host, but a little anxious about animal communication. After the first fifteen minutes of the interview, she jokingly asked me,

"What can you do about termites?"

"Invite them to leave the house," I answered. Mary Ellen was surprised I was so serious.

"I know about communicating with animals, but I never thought about insects," she said.

"They are just trying to stay alive. They eat old wood to nourish their bodies."

"I never thought about that. How would you invite them to leave?" she asked.

"Just think of them as fellow beings; talk to them in words, acknowledge you understand they need nourishment, but explain that you need your house and they are causing damage to it. Offer to make a pile of bark and sticks from the forest behind your house, as a temporary food station during their transition to the woods."

Mary Ellen agreed, and I communicated this to the termites.

We didn't know we are damaging her house; we are just trying to stay alive. We agree to cooperate, and will begin vacating right away. We should be completely out in about a week.

About two weeks later, Mary Ellen phoned me saying she did what I suggested, made a transition pile of wood and bark, and the termites left. The exterminator just left her house and could find no trace of them.

About a month after the show aired, Mary Ellen called me about carpenter ants in her house. I contacted the ants for her. I explained that they were causing damage to her house and she needed her house. I asked them if they would leave. The oversoul of the ants answered me. He explained that they needed to eat wood to keep alive. I offered to have Mary Ellen make a temporary storage of bark and twigs for them next to the house to eat during their transition like she did for the termites. He agreed. I asked the oversoul what it is like to be an ant.

There is much respect and love among us ants for our Queen. We are a group mind, each connected with each other and our Queen. We are in communication with her at all times. We know what we are to do and feel honored to do it.

Each had a sort of genetic programming which gave them the abilities to carry out their work. The oversoul in this case, was like the coordinator of the group, but distinct from the queen. After I explained the problem, they agreed to find another location to live. I was curious if there was any jealousy among them concerning the particular work each was created to perform, so I asked.

Oh, no! Negative attitudes and feelings do not exist at this level of spiritual awareness, only love. We live to serve our Queen and our collective family. We gladly share what we have with each other. Each of us is willing to die for the good and harmony of the group. When we die, our Queen will produce another body for our souls to enter if we wish.

I was very touched by the love among them. It was very humbling to connect with them and experience the intense feeling of love and devotion of these ants for each other and their queen. In the deep recesses of my mind, I couldn't help but wonder if this was the way God intended for humans to live.

The Marriage of Horse and Rider.

Near the end of the week, Becky took me to see her horse, Brighty, whom I had communicated with previously. Brighty was a one-person horse that only speaks to Becky. With Becky's permission, and at long-distance, I asked Brighty if I could talk to her.

Who are you and does my mom know you are talking with me?

I answered yes.

My mom doesn't allow anyone to mess with me or talk with me without her presence.

Brighty contacted Becky, who was on the other end of the phone and said it was all right to talk to Aunt Agnes. She knew I would be coming to New Mexico to visit her in person. When I first saw her, I was taken by her elegance and powerful stance. I asked her, "What is important to you?"

Freedom.

"What do you dream about?"

Being ridden more often.

"Is there a question you would like to ask me?"

How come you don't know about horses?

"When I was young, I didn't have the opportunity, and now my back injuries prohibit it."

Too bad. You are missing a special bonding between horse and rider.

"Tell me about it."

It is a joining of two strong spirits to make a powerful one. This makes both spirits feel complete and something that is much more than they are separately. You think and act as one.

Brighty sent me a picture of a centaur.

Both horse and rider are focused in the same direction.

"Can you send that feeling to me so I experience what you mean?" Brighty sent an impression of me having a strong, powerful body, but my mind seemed quiet and gentle.

"I feel so light."

Yes, like floating, because of so much power, the mind is free to gently float, carefree. The two become fearless, almost invincible.

I felt like a whole new species, with a human mind and a massive, powerful body. We had become a combined unit of flesh and spirit.

All too soon, the week came to an end. There were so many more questions I would have liked to ask. It was an emotional moment when Becky and I said good-bye. I had learned so much from her and her animal companions.

CHAPTER SIX

Shamanism and Telepathic Communication

"While I stood there I saw more than I can tell and understood more than I saw; for I was seeing in a sacred manner the shapes of all things in spirit, and the shape of all things as they must live together like one being."

— The Vision of Black Elk

The following summer, I flew to San Francisco to take an advanced course from Penelope Smith. Penelope is a charming woman, and is recognized as the founder of the interspecies telepathic communication movement. She is the author of several excellent and informative books about animal telepathy. Many of Penelope's readers are grateful for her work, because she took great risk in revealing her skills and abilities to an uninformed public at the time. Now, you can see, read, or hear about animal communicators on television. Ten or twelve years ago that wasn't so. Penelope taught many others the skill. I was excited to be able to study with her.

Days before the class, I received a call from a woman named Vicka Lanier in Billings, Montana, who asked to share a room with me during the workshop. I had already booked a room at the same motel and agreed. It would be fun to have someone to discuss the day's events with. We sent each other photographs so we could find each other at the San Francisco airport. Finally, her plane arrived and we instantly became great friends. Vicka had taken the introductory workshop from Penelope and said she was excited about taking the advanced one this weekend. We rented a car together, and began the two-hour drive to Point Reyes. Fortunately, Vicka was familiar with the area, which helped with the twisted turns of the freeway and up the Francis Drake Highway to the motel. It was a pleasure to get acquainted with her and participate with her in such a learning weekend. We settled down in a cozy room and were eager to begin.

Penelope's dogs royally greeted us as we walked to her house and I lost my footing and slipped on the gravel driveway. Penelope's dog Raya came up to me and said, *Are you OK?* Her communication to me was very clear. "Yes," I said, "Thank you for asking." The house overlooks Point Reyes National Seashore and the view is spectacular. Giant redwood trees line the path up the hill, and the hill is covered with gorgeous evergreens. This year, the workshop consisted of about twelve women. Each gave a little background about herself and how she got into interspecies communication.

One of the women was concerned about the use of animals in research. When it was my turn to speak, I told the group about my experiences with research animals and how the animals themselves felt about it. I asked my animals many years before how they felt about being used in research. They answered by indicating that they knew that they were being incarnated to be used in medical research. They chose this, because they had been treated kindly by humans before (in other lives) and they felt they were making a contribution. The animals' only request was that they be treated kindly, be told in advance what I was planning to do with them, and that they didn't suffer any pain. After my conversation with the rats, I redesigned all my research studies so that they were noninvasive. That is, all studies were performed by naturalistic observation. Everyone at the workshop was surprised by the attitude of the animals. The public is really misinformed about animal research. They only hear horror stories told by the anti-vivisectionists, to shock people into supporting their efforts to curb the use of animals. Some women in the group later told me that I really opened their eyes about how animals feel about participating in research.

Each day Penelope began by offering a Native American-inspired tribute to the Earth Mother, and homage to the powers that be. The first exercise she created for us was to pick an animal that we had not communicated with before, and to talk with it. Penelope has two llamas, one of which I chose to open a conversation with. She told me of her ancestry, and how life was in the Andes; the peace and quiescence of mountain llamas and their herders. I found her to be very enlightened and inspiring. Penelope's pets who talked with the group included Chico San and Sherman, two gorgeous cats who caught my attention. Each day a vegetarian lunch was served and we had the opportunity to move about the grounds. The shore was beautiful and the mountain in the distance majestic.

During one of the "get-in-touch" sessions, we were instructed to contact an animal we didn't like. I chose a particular animal that I was afraid of (a dog). As I spoke with her, she told me about herself. I asked her why she bit me every time she saw me.

I saw you playing with the other dogs and I wanted you to play with me too!

I didn't realize it at the time that I played with the small dogs but unwittingly had left her out. I apologized for my lack of courtesy and the dog sent me warm wishes.

Penelope showed us a way to connect with animals using Shamanic journeying. The word "shaman" is a term to describe a "medicine man" and is used by Native Americans and the tribes of Siberia to signify someone who has access to other spiritual dimensions. Shamans have the power to heal, to make prophecies, to receive visions and to penetrate the mysteries of life and death. They claim to be able to fly and to communicate with animals, nature spirits and the power of life. Shamanism is the oldest form of all spiritual traditions. It has no scriptures, ecclesiastical hierarchies or dogmas, but rather points to the power of life all around us in the organic processes of birth and death. Techniques used to place one in an altered state to effect communication with other dimensions include sky gazing, ancestral drumming, chanting, and sweat lodge purification to name just a few.

For demonstration purposes, Penelope used a drumming technique. I had studied Shamanism with a friend in Cleveland, so I understood the procedure. Communicating with animals by Shamanic Journeying is not the same as telepathic communication. In telepathy, you place yourself mentally on one side of a divide and the being you want to communicate with on the other. There is a bridge that connects the two sides of the divide. You do not cross over the bridge, because the other side exists in another dimension, nor do you allow the being (cat, dog) to cross the bridge over to your side. You stay grounded in this dimension, while contacting the other dimension like talking to a person over the telephone that you can't see physically. If you should cross over the divide, you can still talk to the animal, but when the conversation is ended, you won't remember it. You need to stay grounded in this dimension so that the brain can decode and translate the communication and store it in memory. In telepathy, the telepath is in control of the entire communication. In Shamanic Journeying, one employs the aid of a personal "power animal" who helps guide a person to his or her destination. It is more passive than telepathy. The communicator is passive, allowing only the intention and the guides to help him or her reach his or her destination.

Penelope's methods were very similar to those I learned earlier. She had a beautiful attitude about animals and I could tell that she was very experienced and comfortable with her skills. One thing surprised and intrigued me, and was probably the high point of the workshop. Penelope related that there were "grids" which made up the universe, and how, since childhood, she was able to see these with her physical eyes. This reminded me of what the elk oversoul had told me in New Mexico about the three-dimensional net. Penelope described them, and has written about them in the past. Although I had read all her books, I did not remember reading about this because at the time I did not have a common reference. Since Penelope's workshop I have become aware that much has been written about these grids in the literature of physics, mathematics, and science. The grids appear to form the background fabric of the Universe which makes form possible. One visionary artist, Alex Grey, has painted the grids and published the pictures in his book, *Sacred Mirrors*[1]. He also has made an audio for artists, containing a meditation whereby one is able to see the grids for oneself. I listened to the meditation, and sure enough, I could see the grids when my mind stayed open to them.

As workshop exercises, we spoke telepathically to rocks, plants, trees, mountains, and the ocean. We practiced with rocks and trees in her yard. By that afternoon, my neck and back were hurting so bad from the fall that I needed to lie down. Vicka offered to do a Reiki treatment on my back to relieve the pain. Penelope has in her yard a gazebo-type building which she uses for quiet times and meditation. A few of us went inside. I was not familiar with Reiki at that time but agreed to let Vicka try. Sure enough, my back felt better. This was my first experience with energy healing. In the months following the workshop, Vicka would make appointments in time with me in which she would send Reiki energy to me from Montana to my home in Ohio. She would also send healing energy to my cat Dusty, who claimed that it helped him as well.

During the workshop, Vicka and I took the opportunity to speak with some of the giant redwood trees along Sir Francis Drake Highway. We spotted a giant, regal looking redwood and stopped to speak with it. I didn't know what to ask it, so I just connected with it telepathically and asked if it would share with me some of its experience and perceptions. I sensed the impression of a very old masculine being, like a wise man or sage.

I am hundreds of years old. I live in this place with other beings of my kind. We are very steady, but flexible enough to yield to the power of high winds. You humans are like tiny flickers of light to us, whizzing by so quickly in our time, almost like fireflies in the night. You live your lives rushing to your end, always rushing, never just being. Your lives are over before you even know why you are here. Where is the rush? You will return again and again. Slow down, and take in the beauty of the moment, open your eyes to awareness and take in the wonder of it all. The Earth and everything on it is perfectly made in every detail. Your life will not end without you, so slow down. Just be. When you experience timelessness, you'll understand. Listen quietly, what do you hear?

"I hear the leaves in the trees, some cars nearby, birds chirping, and bees close by, an echo — sounds maybe — like a brook."

Listen longer. Can you hear the heartbeat of the Earth itself generating life? Listen to the air around you with its life-giving breath.

"I don't know if I am in tune with the heartbeat of the Earth, but I definitely can hear the wind and air."

Listen to the whispering song of my leaves as the air passes through them changing the sound as they spring back upon the branches, and wait for another wind to cast their voices.

"What should I do to appreciate what you have to offer?"

Just slow down, contemplate your place in this wonderful show of creation. Allow yourself to be. Join with it.

I thanked the tree for its wise advice, and Vicka and I continued into the quaint village. There were a few small stores selling Wiccan and Celtic mystic articles and some statues of Buddha and of Quan Yin, the divine mother to the Asians. A customer visiting the store brought along her pet wolf. I was naturally attracted to it, and spent some time petting and communicating with it. The wolf had the same sensitive and loving energy as I experienced with Becky's wolves. It appeared to be about three years old. Its owner said she was also a wolf-rescue person, and this one was her newest and favorite wolf.

Later that evening, in the motel room, Vicka and I practiced animal communication with each other's pets. I had the photographs of my cats, and Vicka wanted to try communicating with Peanut. I didn't tell her at first that Peanut was in the spirit world. She was able to "see" him, but asked me about the unusual surroundings, which she described as white lights moving about around him. I explained that Peanut was in the spirit world and the white lights were angels.

"You tricked me," she said.

"Not really," I answered. "I thought you might overcome your block to talking with animals in spirit, if you didn't know Peanut was in the afterlife."

It worked, and Vicka was able to communicate with animals in spirit with ease.

The three-day workshop ended all too soon and Vicka and I left for the airport. We had become very good friends during the trip, and still are today. Vicka practices animal communication and is also a Reiki Master. She practices the Reiki as a healer in her home town of Billings, Montana. When I sent Vicka a draft of this chapter, she asked me to include the following paragraphs:

> It was a joy to meet Agnes and participate with her in such a learning weekend. As Agnes mentioned, I had taken a beginning animal communication workshop previously with Penelope. I hoped to deepen my awareness and telepathic ability during this weekend.

> During one of our "get-in-touch" sessions, we were asked to contact an animal, insect, etc., that we didn't like. Alligators were some of my least favorite beings at that point so I chose them. I connected with an alligator spirit and the experience was very enlightening. I looked through his eyes as he swam lazily on top of the water, and through our conversations grew to understand him and lose my fear of his species. It was a marvelous experience. Perhaps if more of us could understand the creatures that frighten us, the species of the world could get along better.

> Several months after the workshop, I called Agnes for help with one of my four-legged friends. Our dog, Josh, was 13-years-old and getting very sick. The vet said he had congestive heart failure and we knew he wouldn't be with us much longer. So I called Agnes to see how he was doing.

> Even though you may be able to talk to other people's animals, it is often difficult to

communicate with your own. Because of the close emotional and physical attachment, it can be hard to contact them in a detached (objective) way.

So Agnes talked to Josh. She could sense that his inner light was failing and getting very low. Agnes said he knew he would be going shortly and asked us to be with him when he made the transition. Having her help during this traumatic time was so comforting.

We made the tough decision to let Josh go and took him to the vet: he was going downhill so rapidly. My husband and I sat together and held him all through his dying process. As his spirit left his body, I contacted him and he said, "I'm free!" with such joy and excitement. I had to be glad that his spirit was free from the body which caused him so much discomfort and pain.

After we got home from the vet, I contacted Agnes and she got in touch with Josh "on the other side." She said he was with people he had known in past lives. One was a little girl and another was a Native American man. She said he was happy and doing well. I wished him well on his new journey. I was glad he was free of his suffering, but we sure missed him.

— Vicka Lanier

Part Two

CHAPTER SEVEN

How Animals Think

"It was hardly the myth or the message that generated Christianity. It was the attraction of participating in a group experimenting with a new social vision."

Burton L. Mack, *The Lost Gospel:*
The Book of Q & Christian Origins

Human and Non-Human Thought.
Returning home from San Francisco, I looked over my data and discovered striking similarities in the communications of animals, plants, and rocks. But there are distinct differences

How Animals Think

Animals	Humans
Fast answers	Slow answers
Simple answers	Complex answers
Connected with all	Separate from all
Non-judgmental	Judgmental
No dualities	Dualities, polarities
No priorities	Priorities
Timelessness	Time bound
Content benevolent	Content varies
Lives in present	Lives in future/past
Self as spiritual helper	Self as ego
Connected to universe	Self-contained
Eternal	Mortal
All is as it should be	World needs to be fixed
Unified perspective	Singular vantage point
Love, truth, facts	*Preferences, opinions*

between the thoughts of non-human life forms and humans. The most noticeable difference is in the content of communications with non-human life forms, in terms of perception and also attitude. Animals' answers are simple, to the point, have a child-like innocence about them and are predominantly benevolent, loving, and cheerful. Human responses, on the other hand, tend to be guarded, self-centered, and judgmental. I examined this phenomenon more carefully in further communications with both human and non-human life forms over the past ten years.

Unity Consciousness.

Briefly, the world of animals is non-linear, non-dual, non-judgmental and has no space/time concepts. The table shown above gives a summary of the differences between the way animals and humans think. If you look at the left side of the column, it can be seen that the thoughts of animals and other non-human life forms are based upon their awareness of unity, and their connectedness with ALL LIFE. Contrast this with the column on the right, which indicates that the thoughts of humans are based upon their perception of separateness, individuation and selfhood; that is, the body/ego.

Much of the way humans think is based upon their individual cognitive style. By this, I mean that humans express themselves both verbally and behaviorally according to their previous experiences, preferences, and desires. Much of what constitutes the "ego" is a pattern or mold, in which stored knowledge and experiences can be retrieved. The pattern or mold also includes the human "dark side" which the ego protects from being revealed to others at all costs. The "dark side" consists largely of self-judgments and criticisms — such as, selfishness, conceit, ruthlessness, jealousy, fears of inadequacy, superiority and so on. All these dark traits, when properly channeled through the ego are expressed as motivation for success and achievement. What makes the traits "dark" is that the ego is willing to attain its desires regardless of moral costs. To protect the dignity of the ego against recognition of such traits, the mind employs methods of self-deceit. This is accomplished by means of "defense mechanisms" as so elegantly defined by Freud and Jung[1]. Psychoanalytic psychologists define the ego as the personality of the being. As such, retrieval and expression of memories and thoughts must first pass through a "filter" which the ego decides, according to the current situation, is an appropriate response for each occasion, without revealing too much personal information.

Humans have many "hats" that they wear during a single day, including father, son, brother, teacher, husband, lover, neighbor, entrepreneur or worker, and friend. For each of these situations, the amount of the "true person" that is revealed to another person is dependent upon the degree of trust for the other, and the amount of information the person wishes to have known about himself, including his personal feelings, attitudes and opinions. Humans tend to be gullible, since their self-deceit also works well in relation to others, resulting in "blind spots" that prevent the ego from true perception of the other person. Humans have no reliable way to discern truth from falsehood. They are dependent upon their logical appraisal and their gut feelings to distinguish friend from foe. Unfortunately, more often than not, they sway towards logic rather than any intuitive-based feeling which they deem as unreliable. Animals, on the other hand, can read people's intentions, and that gives them a spontaneous, instinctual and accurate determination of friend or foe.

Animals exist in a world in which dualities are transcended. They do not judge or evaluate anything. They just "ARE." They see contrast and opposites as merely degrees within a continuum. For example, where does "hot" become "cold?" At what point do warm and cool become indistinguishable? Animals do not prioritize anything. What about pain and pleasure? If you ask an animal how they are, they will say "fine." If you ask them if they are in pain, they will say, "Yes, my leg is injured." Yes, they may be in pain, but it is not on the top of their list of priorities, because they do not place value judgments on anything, and therefore, no priorities. Pain is simply a part of their overall experience at the moment. Animals live in the present. They do not recognize time/space concepts. Research shows that humans spend 70% of their time worrying about the future; will they have enough money, will their health hold out, will they succeed or fail? Another 20% of their time is spent grieving over the past; did I make the right choices, should I have turned right instead of left, should I regret doing this or that and everyone's favorite, will I be forgiven? Only 10% of their time is spent in the present. The present is all that really exists. The past is gone, and the future is not yet written. It is a waste of 90% of one's mental energy to focus on anything other than the present, because that is where life is really experienced.

The concept of <u>time and space</u> is unknown to animals. These are linear concepts. They live in the present, but have the ability to remember past lives, and in some instances, they are able to tell the future. Animals do understand the concepts of daytime, nighttime, and most important of all, dinnertime, but linear time beyond a few days is foreign to them.

The world of animals is also <u>non-local</u>. Animals rely on energy bands to tell them how close or far away an object is from them. They stay connected to significant others by a sort of telepathic channel. For example, a mother animal is able to keep in constant contact with her offspring by energy bands that connect her with her offspring until she has had the time to prepare them for independent life. Early separation from a mother dog will cause the mother to express loud cries for the pup to return. In cats, the mother will cry out, and then leave her scent around the house for the kitten to find its way home. This can be problematic for pet owners. Premature separation in dogs or cats often results in symbiotic, clinging attachments to the pet owners.
Dogs will whine or bark when its person leaves and continue until its person returns, often upsetting the neighbors, or cats may urinate to mark their territory.

In cats, it is even more complex. Cats have the ability to send out and lay down an energy field of their own. This is true even for big cats living in the wild. The grid protects the house and everything in it, including the humans. It looks similar to the grid of the universe but is localized to the cat's immediate environment. When the grid is disrupted, by entry of a new pet, baby, or even new furniture, the animal becomes confused and disoriented. The cat has to then pull back the energy grid, reorganize it, and lay it back down to include the new or moved item. This takes about three days. It is experienced as a very uncomfortable confusion for the cat and is also hard work. It is like the cognitive dissonance (confusion) one experiences when traveling in a country where traffic is opposite that of the United States. That is, one is forced to drive on the opposite side of the road. One still knows how to drive, but is confused how to make a right turn, and so on. During this time, cats do not slack their responsibility to protect their house. In order to do that, they will urinate in the corners of the room to mark the boundaries. Scent is a more powerful stimulus than the mental energy grids. The way to solve this problem is to let the cat know your comings and goings. Extend them the same courtesy that you would any family member living in the same space.

I received a call about just such a case from a student at Ohio State University. She related to me that her cat was urinating on her textbooks. When I contacted the cat, it seemed really "pissed off." I asked if the student had brought something new into the apartment. She acknowledged that she had a new puppy. The cat said, *I want you to tell me when you change something in the house!* The student said, "Okay, okay." The cat continued, *I want you to talk to me in words!* "Okay, but why are you peeing on my books?" *Because THAT'S WHERE THE WORDS ARE!* Animals will try to communicate with you in body language or in symbolic language to get their point across. They act out a sort of pantomime, until they figure out the least amount of cues they will need to get their owners to do what they want. Some common examples are the dogs getting their leash, or cats bringing empty bowls to their persons, or pawing cabinet doors or closets where their toys are being stored.

Communications with animals are always <u>benevolent</u>. Animals believe that everything is happening in and of itself, that neither humans nor non-human beings cause anything to happen. Animals say that the universe doesn't make any mistakes, that everything is exactly the way it is supposed to be. For animals, life is the natural evolutionary expression of the one life (All That Is). For example, animals understand their missions.

I had a call from a man who wanted to connect with a dog in the spirit world. The pet lived with him when the man was in his twenties. According to the gentleman, he was unkind to the pet, beating him often with a newspaper and wanted to ask the animal for forgiveness.

The dog communicated to me that there was no need for the apology, because it was part of his mission to go through that experience for the benefit of the person. When I queried the dog further, it communicated that its mission with this person was to bear the cruelty so his person could learn regret, guilt, remorse, and compassion. I am often astounded by the great lengths our animal companions will go to help us on our spiritual path.

Facts Versus Opinions.

> *"Mojave Dan broke his silence...'There's facts about dogs and there's opinions. If you want the facts get them straight from the dog; if you want opinions, ask Humans.'"*
>
> J. Allen Boone, *Kinship With All Life*[2]

Because animals are totally connected to ALL, they are able to see all sides of an issue and understand that everything is the way it should be. Humans, operating from a singular vantage point, believe that their viewpoint and perspective is the correct one, and all others should follow suit. For humans, the world needs to be fixed. As an illustration, consider a holographic picture. There are tiny grooves in the covering surface, which cause light to be bent in different ways. Although the picture is stationary, as one moves slowly past the picture, light bends with the grooves causing a distortion of the original picture. It looks different. For humans, this conflict will invoke a re-evaluation of the picture and its content. At each vantage point as you pass by the picture, the light causes the picture to change and elicits another re-evaluation. Thus, interpretation of the content of the picture is a function of the person's state of awareness and the observer's vantage point.

Return to the table. The left column can be summarized in three words: love, truth and facts. The right column can be summarized in two words: preferences and opinions.

Is the Ego Really so Bad?

In recent years, the ego has really been getting a bad rap. Sometimes you feel guilty for even having a mind of your own. What is the alternative, total passivity? No. The ego serves a valuable purpose. It is necessary for the survival of humans to be constantly aware of their surroundings. This includes protection from the harsh elements, being able to select which foods are safe to eat and being aware of present dangers.

Humans have the gift of creativity, as well. In order to create anything, it is necessary to make value judgments and establish a hierarchy of priorities. For example, people cannot conceive of the color gray without awareness of its opposite poles, white and black. Humans are able to make fine discriminations between points on a continuum and synthesize and blend existing things together to create new ones.

Consider the farming and agricultural industries. Almost everything is a product of selective breeding, including the plants that yield the best crops, the grass, and the heartiest livestock that will be used for human consumption to provide maximum nourishment without harmful by-products. If we reincarnate over and over, as animals say we do, and as many religions believe, then it follows that an ego would be necessary to recreate a person within a new context (or time period). Being an efficient sheep herder in Australia in a prior life would not necessarily be a skill needed to be an efficient news analyst in New York today.

It is the job of the ego to pick and choose what the human will become within the current context. Once the ego is formed it is no longer the exclusive designer of its own destiny. The ego can be set aside to incorporate into a human's personality the esoteric characteristics of kindness, compassion, sincerity, loyalty, honesty, spontaneity, and love. This openness to the wonders of the universe is also the doorway to understanding the divine. By recognizing kinship with ALL LIFE, a person recognizes the divinity in all things, including himself or herself. This awareness sparks both humility and gratitude for being a part of it all. As the animals say, everything is the perfect unfolding expression of what it was meant to be. Animals do not experience separation, dualities and contrast. I asked animals about this. Dusty Rose, Becky's wolf in the afterlife, said it is because animals see and act for the good of the whole group. Humans use the concept of separation for personal gain.

The human perceptions of <u>separation</u>, <u>polarities</u> and <u>opposites</u> have been with us since recorded history. Was it not first told in the Biblical story of Adam and Eve? Supposedly, the pair lived in Paradise, without need or want. They were one with the universe and the Creator. The Creator warns them not to eat the fruit of the tree of the knowledge of good and evil, but does not say why. The tree of the knowledge of good and evil appears to be man's earliest experience with separation, contrast, polarities and opposites. When the pair eats the fruit, they realize they are no longer one with the universe, but rather, they are separate from the Creator. They recognize their nakedness and try to hide. Enter the human ego and its defense mechanisms to hide the supposed shame and fear of disobeying the Creator's instructions. The Creator then casts them out of Paradise to toil and create for themselves all the things necessary for survival and growth on a hostile earth.

Animals stayed in the land of unity with The Creator. They don't see themselves as separate. They are still one with All That Is. The table provides a glimpse of what it must have been like to live in Paradise before the fall. Part of us still does. Animals are here to remind us of that.

An Animal's Job or Purpose.

All animals are here to help their persons on their spiritual journey. When I questioned the animals about what this meant, I received almost the same answer from each animal. The following is a composite:

Humans have been invited to be the co-creators of their own species and their own world. Humans once were life forms similar to ours, but some advanced more than other animals, showing them to be capable of self-restraint and making good choices. Because of this, the Creator of All gave humans the perception of separateness, individuation, and self-awareness. Animals are excited about this. We do everything we can to provide love, support and encouragement to our persons to that end. We teach them the things they need to know in order to carry out their missions.

"Like what?"

We teach patience, loyalty, humility, acceptance of others, and being able to see the whole rather than just parts of a situation.

"What do you mean by the whole?"

As animals, seeing ourselves as connected to all life, we are able to see all sides of an issue or problem. Unfortunately, because you humans see yourselves as separate, you can only see one side of the story — your side. There are no real differences of opinions, just misunderstandings that arise because you are only looking at one side of the story. We can initiate situations ourselves, often with our own bodies to send these messages to you, for learning. We animals understand this, and give you unconditional love and assurance so that you continue co-creating. We are honored to do this.

"Can you give me an example?"

Sometimes we come into this life with a defect like blindness or deafness, or even lameness. By our gentle and loving example, we help you realize that nothing is perfect, but still capable of giving and receiving love, and that if we can overcome our handicap and still be happy and playful, that our person can too! It is more of an inspiration example for humans rather than a teaching. Sometimes our job is to keep people on their toes by being playful rascals, so our person does not give up on life. Other times, we keep old people healthy by making them exercise, you know, by making them take us for walks. That is our job!

CHAPTER EIGHT

Pet Truths

Animal communication provides a privileged insight not only into the mind of animals, but gives the communicator a glimpse of a higher spiritual realm. It is a peek into a world of benevolence, simplicity, non-duality, and complete mutual understanding. It is a portal to what mystic writers call the "universal mind."

I spent twenty-five years in the laboratory studying the way animals learn and think. These studies never prepared me for what I was about to learn by talking to animals directly. Communicating with thousands of animals, and in the spirit of the scientific method, I asked each animal the same questions. Their answers surprised me and introduced me to a whole new realm of thought. Some of their statements were so sophisticated that I found it necessary to research their answers to determine if what they said could possibly be true. It always was. After a time, I came to call these "Pet Truths."

These truisms are what prompted me to write this book. The phenomenon is not simply communicating with an animal because there are over 4,000 animal communicators listed on the Internet alone that can do the same thing. The real phenomenon is what animals have to say if asked the right questions. This is where my clinical interviewing skills came in handy. I asked some of life's bigger questions, and found that animals have access to a wealth of knowledge about their own bodies and what is going on in our human minds. They possess a thorough understanding of life, death, reincarnation, and how the universe works.

Because animals are non-biased, not religiously or politically slanted, non-judgmental, and do not have any vested interest in the information they give, they are the best teachers in the world. They are not limited to the linear world of time/space events. They simply ARE! They exist in the present. Animals experience life, in just the way it comes, without avoidance of the negatives, including pain and aging. Humans tend to think about life. In this way, they analyze all incoming sensory data and process it in order to avoid pain (both mental and physical) and maximize pleasure and success.

Below are some examples of simple Pet Truths.

Pet Truth #1: We are all connected.

Q. How do you know so much about the Universe?

A. *You humans believe yourselves to be separate beings. Animals know we are one. We are all connected with every other life form — humans, animals, plants, rocks, oceans, and even Mother Earth herself. We are all a living, evolving expression of the one life. We call it, All That Is.*

Q. In what way do you connect?

A. *We are connected by an invisible band of energy which we call the heart connection. It is energy of pure love. It is energy of deep attraction and attachment. It holds the entire cosmos together. It looks like a web. Some humans call it the Ether. We call it the heart connection.*

COMMENTARY:

I found this hard to believe, but I researched this and found it to be true.

Physicist David Bohm[1] calls these energy bands the "implicate" or unmanifested order and "explicate" or manifested order. To Bohm, the entire universe is set up in an orderly way. The "implicate" or implied order consists of bands of energy that act as a background pattern for every possible object to become manifest in the physical dimension. Conceptualize it as akin to a computer game where all the possible outcomes have been provided, and the player is in control of the outcome of this particular play. Deepak Chopra calls it the "field of pure potentiality[2]." Biologist Rupert Sheldrake[3, 4] discovered these bands of energy, which he termed "morphogenetic fields," (meaning the evolution and development of form).

Sheldrake's work began because of a curiosity of the behavior of homing pigeons. In his research, he found that pigeons find their way home or to their point of origin by certain bands of energy which act as channels for telepathic communication. He found that these invisible bands connect an animal to its home, a person, or other animals. It allows them to find their way home over great distances, even over unfamiliar terrain. These bands are what link animals to objects of their intention (e.g., going home) and also their attention (e.g., their person). The bands appear to vary in size, length, and intensity, and can even be what holds an organism in mutual cooperation with its components.

Lynn McTaggert[5], an award-winning investigative journalist, claims these energy bands are what allow communication from one cell to another, cell to organ, or cell to brain. All cells within the entire body are in constant communication with all other parts so that the needs of a single cell can be attended to by each organ system and the brain.

Bruce Cathie[6], a commercial pilot, investigated and worked out the mathematics of what he calls the energy grid. Visionary artist Alex Grey[7] has painted the grid, and published some of his work in the book *Sacred Mirrors*. Grey has also produced a meditation for artists that guide the person into recognizing the existence of the grid through visualization technique[8]. I have listened to the tapes and found them to be very effective in seeing and recognizing the grids for the first time.

J. Allen Boone, a journalist and movie producer who was transformed by his experience with Strongheart, the actor-dog, has made animal-human relationships his life work[9, 10, 11]. Boone relates his discovery:

"Behind every object which the senses can identify, whether the object is human, animal, tree, mountain, plant or anything else and right where the object seems to be, is the mental and spiritual fact functioning in all its completeness and perfection. This spiritual fact surrounds the object on all sides, and is in intimate contact with every other object. This spiritual fact cannot be recognized with ordinary human eyesight but is always apparent to clarified inner vision[12]."

This "aura" is evident in Kirilian photography. Today, there are even computer programs that can photograph and videotape the energy field around living objects, including humans.

Animals are aware of the energy grid and the aura. They simply call it the *heart connection*. When an animal communicator enters the "telepathic field," the grids become apparent. The *heart connection* is the energy band that connects one being with another. It is easily seen with *inner vision*. I can best describe it as being like a distortion of air above a heat source — like a candle. As the flame warms the air around it, the air expands and also rises. As it does, the light will bend as it hits the warmed air, causing the objects behind the air to look distorted. When the communicator connects to the client, usually over the telephone, the communicator follows the heart connection from the client to the animal. When the animal is located, the communicator is then able to see everything the animal is connected with. This will include family members, other animals in the home, and even persons in the animal's previous homes. If queried about its species, the animal will show you the net-like connection with all other members of the species, and even other species.

The significance of the *heart connection* in the ability of psychics to communicate with a person's deceased relatives in the afterlife was studied by Gary E. Schwartz, Ph.D. at the University of Arizona for an HBO television documentary in which psychic phenomena were addressed using traditional physiological recording methods[13-15]. The consistent finding among all five psychics tested is that the activity of the heart of the psychic (pattern A) changed when the psychic "tuned in" to the test subject (pattern B). When the psychic detected the presence of a spirit entity (who identified himself as the test subject's deceased husband) coming through, the heart activity of the psychic changed a second time when communication with the sentient being commenced (pattern C). These studies are discussed further in Chapters 9 and 10.

Pet Truth #2: Animals read your intentions.

Q. Can animals read people's minds?

A. *Yes, but not in the way you think about it. You humans have so much chatter going on in your minds all the time it would be very hard to listen to all of it. What we read is your intentions. When you arrive at a decision to do something that will affect us, we know what you are planning at that instant.*

Q. Can you give me an example?

A. *Yes. We know when you are planning to leave the house, and where you are going. We know when you are going to take us to the vet. We know when you intend to give us dinner, and when you are going to bed. We know events in the future, like if you are planning to move.*

COMMENTARY:

Evidence from electroencephalography (EEG) recordings from human subjects indicates that when at rest, humans have a lot of random activity in the brain. When thought becomes focused as in concentrating, speaking, or in performing an activity, brain waves become synchronized. *Intention* appears to be the most significant factors in telepathic communication, and in the way one is able to influence outcomes. For example, Sheldrake studied the behavior of animals to determine how an animal knows his person is on the way home. Subjects in his study were told to synchronize their watches with an observer at home. Another observer followed the subject to various destinations, by various transportation methods (a truck, bus, car, walking, etc.). He found that at the exact time a person sets his intention to return home, the animal will respond by waiting at the front door, etc.

Many animals say that we humans never relax: that is, we think too much of the time and that is what prevents us from hearing their communications to us. Intuitive and psychic abilities are believed to be a function of the right side of the brain, while language appears to be restricted to left brain activity. Lesions or damage to the left brain will result in a variety of symptoms involving verbal communication of thought. Students of mystic schools are encouraged to develop right brain intuitive abilities through a variety of methods. The most common of these is deep meditation, during which a person focuses intention on breathing and gently allows random thoughts to come and go. Some instructors request students wait and pay attention to their next thought.

Try this now. If you wait for a thought to appear, you will wait a long time. The purpose of meditation is to eliminate the constant brain activity associated with language. When communicating with animals, telepaths must first quiet their mind and enter an altered state, which is nothing more than a meditative state. Once language is pushed aside, the telepathic field is entered and impressions are received by the intuitive or right side of the brain. As I described earlier, telepathic communication is reception of an "impression" which then has to be filtered up through the brain and translated into language. The impression is received in about one ten-thousandth of a second, whereas the conversion to language may take several minutes[16]. To produce a single sentence, the brain must access memory data banks to locate the appropriate symbol and words to accurately describe the contents and meaning of the impression.

Pet Truth #3: Animals do not make judgments.

Q. Do you think humans are good or evil?

A. *Animals do not think in those terms. We exist in the realm of non-duality. By this I mean that we do not experience dualities or polarities like good vs. evil, strong vs. weak, love vs. hate, best vs. worst, pain vs. pleasure. These are merely different degrees of the same thing. Such ideas require a value judgment, which we do not do. Since we are connected to everything, we understand all sides of the picture or story. You humans believe yourselves to be separate, so you can see only your side of the story. You define good or evil according to how it affects you — personally. If it is in your best interest and promotes your goal, you call it good; if it interferes with your goals, you call it evil. In truth, there are no rights or wrongs. You humans make judgments according to your unique view of the world at the time, because your view takes into consideration factors from only a singular perspective. Animals see all sides and have no need to judge anything.*

Q. You know when you are in pain, don't you?

A. *Yes, of course. But we do not dwell on pain like you humans do, because that would require placing a value or priority on pain. That requires judgment, which we don't do. Pain is simply a sensation that we feel, along with many other sensations. We do not place a value on it, nor an emotion. It simply IS.*

COMMENTARY:

This was a difficult concept to understand. Because humans see themselves as separate, we tend to place value judgments and prioritize everything based upon our own preferences. If you ask an animal how it feels, it will answer "fine." If you then ask the same animal if it is in pain, it will say something like, "Yes, my foot is broken." When inquiring into an animal's state of health, be very specific. For example, I will ask the animal to show me his body. Because of my long experience with laboratory animals, it will send me a 3-dimensional image of its body resembling an x-ray film. Then I will scope the image to detect obvious abnormalities like broken bones, tumors, etc. As I carefully screen for problems, the animal may tell me where any discomfort or pressure is located. I once asked my very dearest cat Dusty how he felt. He answered, *Just ode* (old), *this is what it feels like to be ode* (old). Animals experience life in whatever manner it comes.

Researching the concept of non-duality, several references from the spiritual literature supported the animals' explanations. *The Kybalion*[17] provides a very good description of the concept of non-polarities — that all things exist on a continuum. For example, when people think of hot versus cold, they explain that they are merely degrees of the same thing. Where does hot become cool and cold become warm? In perceptual psychology, researchers describe what they term "just noticeable differences" (JNDs). Subjects are asked to identify when a sensory stimulus placed on the arm or other part of the body is detected as different from the previous stimulus. Findings indicate that JNDs are exponentially detected. That is, a temperature probe may be perceived as warm at 99 degrees Fahrenheit, where the probe will have to reach 110 degrees before a JND is detected. The concept of judgment and singular vantage points is eloquently described in the book, *The Eye of the I* by David Hawkins, M.D., Ph.D.[18], and will not be presented here.

Pet Truth #4: Animals have the capacity for creative thought.

> Q. To a white cockatoo with one damaged wing: What would you like most in the world?
>
> A. This beautiful bird sent three visual images. The first was an image of his head, with wind blowing against his face causing his feathers to ruffle. The second was an image of him with his feet strapped to the luggage rack on the top of a moving automobile, feeling the breeze as it moved along. The third was an image of him riding on the back of a horse in a round arena. When the horse stopped, someone came over and put a wreath around the horse's neck for the bird. The cockatoo said, *If given the chance, I could fly so fast, I would win a prize!*

COMMENTARY:

Since the cockatoo's wing was damaged, he could no longer fly on his own. The bird used end-point analysis (flying fast) and creative thinking to devise a new way to accomplish the same goal. Animals do not have the concepts of speed or distance; these are space/time events. The bird's goal was to experience the sensation of flying fast with the wind or breeze blowing through his feathers. Riding on top of a car or horse would accomplish the same thing.

Compare this with the work of behavioral scientists like B.F. Skinner[19]. Skinner believed that animal learning was only stimulus-response pairings. He found he could train any animal to do anything by controlling the reinforcements (usually a pellet of food). Through successive approximations, Skinner was able to shape a behavior. For example, to train a dog to jump for a morsel of food, he would first reinforce the dog by giving it a food morsel for just holding its head up. Then he would withhold the food pellet until the dog lifted his front paws off the floor. Next, he would raise the food pellet higher and higher until the dog jumped off the ground to get it. He termed this type of learning "operant conditioning."

In contrast, Russian physiologist, Ivan Pavlov, believed that animals were capable of motivation. His method involved using the autonomic nervous system to produce stimulus-response and stimulus-stimulus pairings. Pavlov prepared a dog surgically so that the vessels of salivary glands of the dog's mouth were exteriorized from the skin. On the end of the vessel, he placed a small tube to collect saliva. He then put a meat powder on the dog's tongue, and the dog salivated. He was able to pair this with the sound of a bell, so that the sound of the bell alone produced salivation. To his surprise, the dog salivated to just about any environmental cue associated with the test room. The degree to which the dog salivated was directly related to the amount of time the dog was deprived of food. The longer the deprivation, the less it would take to trigger the salivation. He termed this "classical conditioning."

These two methods are the ones primarily used in laboratory studies to determine how animals learn and think. In the example of the cockatoo presented above, the bird clearly was not conditioned in any way to riding a horse, or riding on the top of a car with its feet strapped to the luggage rack. The cockatoo's communication indicates that it is observant of the world around it, and it has the ability to put things together in a unique way to solve its problem of the broken wing and artificially produce the experience of flight.

Pet Truth #5: Pets have a mission in life.

Q. Do you know how much everyone loves you?

A. *I am supposed to have them love me. That is my mission in life.*

Q. Your mission?

A. *Yes. All animals have a mission. We are here to help humans on their spiritual journey. Our general mission is to give unconditional love and acceptance. Then we have a particular mission for our person. That depends upon his or her particular needs in life. You humans may or may not know your particular mission in life, but we know it because we are part of it.*

COMMENTARY:

I have asked hundreds of animals what their particular mission is. The answers vary from "to keep their persons healthy by making them take me for a walk" or "to guard the children," to "keep you on your toes." Each one has a different mission. Some animals have more than one. Pets adopted from shelters often have a mission with their first families and a completely different one with their current families. Sick animals will often cling to life until their mission is completed.

Some animals will tell you what their mission is, and some won't. Here is a tender story of a beautiful greyhound named Zoey and her mission.

Zoey's mission. Animals are the best spiritual teachers ever! Peggy Kostelnik heard through a friend I was able to communicate with animals telepathically. She called me one evening about her eight-year-old greyhound, Zoey, who was diagnosed with cancer in her right front leg. Peggy asked if Zoey needed to be put down by the vet. I contacted Zoey telepathically, whose answer was *No! I am not finished with my mission yet. I am not ready to leave.*

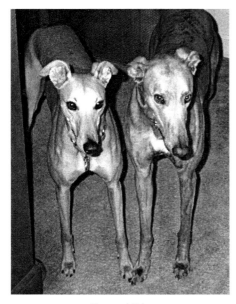

Zoey and Zeke

Zoey sent me an image of her body with her right leg definitely revealing a golf-ball sized growth at the ankle. Her energy level was like that of a young animal. *I think the cancer is localized to only one area of my body, just at my ankle.*

I asked Peggy if a biopsy of the growth was taken to determine the cell type of the cancer. She replied the diagnosis was by x-ray alone. Being a scientist, I am more comfortable with actual test data. "Until you have a biopsy, the diagnosis is merely anecdotal — an opinion," I said. I recommended Zoey be seen by a veterinary oncologist in the area. It is best to ask animals what they want to do. Peggy thought it was a good idea and called for an appointment. To prepare Zoey for the visit, I explained what a biopsy was and how it would be done.

A few days later, Peggy called to let me know that the biopsy was positive for osteosarcoma, a deadly cancer of the bone. However, new x-rays indicated that it was localized to the right leg. The veterinarian had three options for Peggy to consider, which I communicated to Zoey: she could do nothing and let the cancer take its course until she passed away; be put down now and avoid the progression of the disease; and she could choose to undergo surgical removal of her right leg and receive chemotherapy afterwards to destroy any cancer cells that may have traveled somewhere else in her body. *I choose the surgery. I am not finished with my mission. I think I am going to be around for some time yet.* Peggy honored Zoey's decision. I communicated to Zoey details of how the surgery would be performed and how she would be re-trained to walk on three legs. She understood and agreed.

The surgery was successful and no cancer was found in Zoey's lymph nodes, confirming it was localized to the right leg, just as Zoey said! The day after surgery, Peggy was permitted to visit her. She called me from her cell phone outside the vet hospital before going in. I contacted Zoey, who appeared alert, happy, and excited that Peggy was coming to see her. *I hope my mommy is not startled by my appearance. I want her to look beyond what she sees on the surface and see me as a complete being, despite my missing leg.*

When Peggy entered the visitation room, Zoey walked in on her three legs. Peggy was prepared to see her this way, since I related Zoey's communication to her.

In the following weeks, Peggy called me with several updates on Zoey's condition. Zoey healed completely and was receiving chemotherapy. I connected with her.

Now I can tell you what my mission is.

"We have been wondering,"

My mission is to help Mommy and her family to look beyond the physical aspects of a being, and be able to recognize the spiritual essence behind my physical form. I am still the same being I was, my spiritual body is the same, only my physical form has changed. I still give Mommy and her family and Zeke (a second greyhound) *the same love and companionship as before. Life in a body is never perfect, only the soul is perfect. Mommy needed to know this for a new career path she will find. I will be her assistant. Together, we will help sick people to realize their full potential and joy in life.*

Zoey lived another nine months, and during that time, Peggy's brother succumbed to cancer. Because of Zoey, Peggy was able to give her brother the understanding he needed to still see himself as whole.

Zoey died later that year and the following year, her long-time playmate Zeke contracted osteosarcoma of the limbs as well. When I contacted Zeke in the afterlife, he said he was with Zoey again. I asked him to show me how he entered the afterlife. Zeke showed me that after he received the shot from the vet, he floated up above his body. A male angel who looked like a boy about four years old climbed on his back and rode Zeke into the afterlife. Zeke was a professional greyhound race dog, and he told me that he witnessed horses and riders in the stables and wanted to see what it would be like to have someone ride him like a horse. The angel understood his wish and accommodated him.

Pet Truth #6: Pets give you unconditional love.

Q. Can you explain to me what unconditional love really means? I can feel it, but I am not sure how you think about it.

A. *It is simply this: truth and love without judgment. It is the non-judgment that counts.*

Q. Do you give everyone that same kind of love?

A. *I think you are confusing love with bonding. We love all life: we bond to certain persons or animals.*

COMMENTARY:

Perhaps unconditional love is really the only kind of love there is. Animals claim that love is energy that holds all things together. If one considers the energy bands described in Pet Truth # 1, maybe what humans call love is not a subjective experience at all, but the background fabric that holds together that which we call the universe. Taken one step further, it may be that God or the Creator itself is that life force. Religious text tells us that "God is Love," but does not teach us what that really means. Animals refer to the Creator as *All That Is*, meaning everything in existence. When humans connect telepathically with the energy grid, they observe that it extends vertically, horizontally, and transversely in every direction as far as one can see (or even comprehend). When I ask animals to show me their perception of God, what I receive is a white light that seems to come from everywhere and extends into infinity. Can it be that energy is love and that unconditional love is energy without barriers?

What makes unconditional love so special in animals seems to be the recognition that the feeling is sincere (true) and not masked, and totally without judgment. There is something about the human soul that recognizes truth. Animals say that when we experience the subjective feeling of love, we are recognizing or remembering who we really are — spirit. Then how does conditional love fit in? Even though humans adore their pets, there are certain expectations (like using the litter box) that go along with that love, making it conditional even if only in a small way. A mother unconditionally loves her child and at the same time she can disapprove of a specific behavior like pulling the dog's ears. When communicating with an animal and its person, you can "see" with inner vision a radiance of warmth and attachment between the two, and it appears, at least to the telepath, to be the same. Perhaps at the level of spirit, instead of ego, it is the same.

Pet Truth #7: Animals in groups think and act as a group mind, with an oversoul.

Below is a description of a communication with a herd of elk in New Mexico. When talking with a herd, you imagine a web-like structure, like a net covering the entire herd. They have a group mind. You talk to the group, and the oversoul will answer.

Q. Do you know that the Forestry Service is planning on doing construction on this site?

A. *Thank you for your concern. We have been
aware all along, because we are in communication
with all life, including humans. We have loved
this valley, but we understand what the Forestry
Service is trying to do. We have selected several other
spots in the mountains where we can go when the
construction begins. Just as you saw the net covering
us, there is a net that covers all life on this planet.
We shared our needs with other wildlife and the rams
have agreed to open their space for us to enter.*

COMMENTARY:

Professor Sheldrake spent many years trying to understand
the behavior of homing pigeons and other flocks of birds.
Many scientists theorized that it was scent, a kind of radar, or
some other silent energy that enables birds to fly in unison. The
explanation given to me by the oversoul elk seems to be the best
that has been offered. When one connects with the telepathic
field, the net-like structure which connects the herd or group
can be seen with inner vision. It makes sense to me that if herds
and flocks of animals operate as a group mind, then the leader
can direct them successfully. Sheldrake studied this phenomenon
and discovered that pigeons that belong to a group living in the
same home (like a wooden coop), when released, will navigate
in unison and return to the wooden coop even when it is
moved miles away. Sheldrake made a video to demonstrate this
phenomenon in pigeons, in "Seven Experiments That Could
Change the World[20, 21]." It is truly remarkable to see how pigeons
who seemingly flew off into the distance, away from the flock,
are called back to the flock once the new location of the coop is
discovered by the oversoul.

There appears to be something in this universe that makes
order out of chaos. Humans seem to be drifting further and
further apart from one another. Yet, in times of crisis, like the
9/11 attack on the World Trade Center, something in each of
us around the world unites. It is like the conditional love of the
mother example above. We hold to our judgments, criticisms,

and disapprovals, but when the chips are down, we seem to unite. What affects any one of us appears to affect us all.

It has been said that radio and television made the world smaller. Yet, it appears that the most significant progress of uniting those of us who share this planet is the Internet. Information is available to anyone by the touch of a finger within seconds. Is the Internet the "implicate order" as described by Bohm, Sheldrake and others?

CHAPTER NINE

Death and Dying

Do Animals Have Souls?

Many people ask me that question. The answer is definitely YES! Not only have I learned animals have souls, but they are actually part of our energy, part of our own souls. All animals are here to help their persons with their spiritual journey. They can reincarnate and return to us, and they have been with us in every lifetime in one form or another.

What is a soul and how is it measured? It is the non-physical aspect of a being which expresses itself as the attitude, emotions, moral aspects and will of a being which distinguishes the being as an entity distinct from physical form.

One of the best descriptions of a soul or spirit is contained in J. Allen Boone's book, *Kinship With All Life*[1], published in 1954. Boone was a movie producer who spent several months pet-sitting for an actor-dog named Strongheart. Boone was fascinated with Strongheart because he appeared to understand the scripts of the film being produced. At first, Boone related to Strongheart as man versus dog, and Strongheart communicated with him in a kind of pantomime. After a while, Boone became attached to Strongheart and began to see him in a different light — as a fellow being. From then on, Boone began receiving communications from Strongheart which he instantly recognized as thought transfer. Boone had many deep conversations with Strongheart and began to receive communications from other beings. He discovered that the same spiritual essence he found in animals could also be found in every object including plants, trees, rocks, mountains, and everything else in creation.

> "If one took the time to look beyond the apparent features seen with their physical eyes, with an open mind and heart, one could also 'see' with

inner vision a spiritual fact just behind each object which existed in its entire wholeness. This spiritual fact (or essence) extended beyond the boundaries of the object on every side and was in intimate contact with every other object in creation as well."

The human energy field. Contemporary researchers like Valerie Hunt[2] refer to this spiritual essence as the *human energy field* (HEF) in humans, and the *energy field* (EF) in non-humans and other biological life. Hunt measured the *human energy field* under research laboratory conditions. She used special sensing devices called electrodes which are long needles insulated except at the cut tip that are commonly used to perform electromyography (EMG) in patients with muscle dysfunction. Hunt noticed that even before she put the needle electrodes into a human muscle, her oscilloscope was detecting a signal that was lower in amplitude (intensity) and higher in frequency than that found in muscle. She designed an experiment to study this strange signal. Hunt's subjects were people who could see auras. She asked them to describe auras and asked the subjects to describe its location (surrounding the body). When all the subjects agreed how far away from the body the aura extended, she employed a micro manipulator to advance the needle, and had the subjects confirm when the tip of the needle electrode entered the HEF, or aura. The subjects reported seeing different colors within the aura. Hunt recorded from the electrical field within each color of the aura, and found that each color corresponded to a different amplitude and frequency. She also measured the frequencies of areas along the midline of the body which energy workers refer to as "Chakras." She reports that skeletal muscle vibrates about 250 cycles per second (cps). When people are concentrating on the physical plane of existence, their HEF vibrates at the same frequency as skeletal muscle, 250 cps. When people are thinking about more spiritual or esoteric matters, their vibrations increase to about 400 and as high as 900 cps. She also found that among mediums, while in trance, the HEF vibrates in a narrow range between 800 and 900 cps. She has measured people whom she terms "mystics" with vibrations up to 15,000 cps, and even some persons up to 200,000 cps. Her results correspond with some religious beliefs that explain spiritual growth as "raising your level of vibrations." There are computer programs that can detect auras and project them onto a computer screen. As people are instructed to think of different objects or persons, the aura is seen to change. For example, if the subject thinks of someone they love, the aura changes to yellow and light purple, whereas when thinking of someone they are angry toward, the aura exhibits dark reds or blues.

Barbara Brennan, an associate of Hunt's and a participant in one of her studies, expanded on her work, and used it to form the basis of her book, "Hands of Light[3]." Brennan demonstrated a method of healing allowing the universal energy to flow through the healer's hands and modify the patient's HEF, bringing about corresponding changes in the patient's physical body. Brennan concludes that humans are not a body with a spirit inside them, but a spirit with a body inside them.

Further evidence for an *energy* field surrounding every object comes from a phenomenon known as Kirilian photography. This is a special photographic technique in which an aura of light radiating from the object is captured on film. Thus, the spiritual essence of beings, plants, and even rocks can be objectively seen, photographed, and measured. The most convincing evidence of an *energy field* surrounding the object comes from a demonstration of the phenomenon in which a leaf is cut in half, and the spiritual essence of the leaf is still glowing in full form without the presence of the physical portion of the leaf, which has been removed. This *energy field* has been captured by Kirilian photography surrounding a human hand as well.

The soul — a ball of white light. Recall from Chapter 1 the story of my communication with the Shelty. When I explained to the Shelty how unsure of myself I was around dogs, and asked how I might overcome this, he answered, *Just get to know us better.*

Then he said, *I'll show you*. He sent me an image of a ball of pure white light energy about the size of his body. The ball looked like the nucleus of an atom, with electrons speeding to and fro all around it and radiating out from it in every direction. It looked similar to pictures of the surface of the sun with its constant eruptions. The minute I saw the ball of white light, I subjectively recognized it as the same soul that exists in all of us. No words were needed. I just "knew." At that moment, all my fears and doubts disappeared. I felt a kinship with all dogs everywhere.

One of the exercises that I present to students taking my workshops is to talk to an animal and ask it questions with deep meaning. One question that always comes up is, "Will you show me what your soul looks like?" It is amazing, that among the 15 or so persons attending a workshop, and all asking a single animal, all 15 students will describe receiving an image of a white ball of light in answer to the question. Likewise, if there are 15 dogs or cats, and each of the 15 students selects only one animal to ask, the answer will still be the same — a ball of white light.

Yes, animals certainly do have souls, and it appears that all objects in the physical dimension do as well. Animals tell me that many souls can be part of the same energy, that is, the same being. They explain that is how they are able to reincarnate and come back to their person again and again. Animals are a part of our own soul. Attractor patterns are patterns of attachment between beings. These are set up by one's karmic past and preferences as described by Hunt[4]. These attractions keep your pets and other loved ones returning to us in every lifetime, in one form or another.

Attachment and Loss.

Ask anyone who has ever had a pet and they will tell you that the loss of an animal, whether through death or other forms of separation, is one of the most painful events a human being can experience. Because animals often are totally dependent upon their persons for their very survival, humans tend to feel completely responsible for everything that happens to them. If the pet is ill, the person often will blame themselves for not being aware of the animal's stress and will look for things they may have done wrong in their care. Feelings of guilt are often expressed in statements like, "If I had taken him to the vet sooner," or "I didn't pay enough attention when the dog was barking, he must have been trying to tell me he was in pain." The person may wish that he or she could somehow magically turn back the clock, be there moments before the fatal event, and alter the outcome.

I have spoken to hundreds of animals in spirit form in the afterlife. Animals say that the universe doesn't make mistakes and everything is the way it should be. Their death is no exception. They leave the physical world at the exact moment they are supposed to and not one moment before. Animals say they send intuitive messages to their persons so that they always know if it is time for the animal to depart. Animals do not leave the physical dimension until their mission is completed, even if it means that they will suffer for a time. There is one exception, in the event that an animal is put down or killed, as an act of revenge of one being to another. For example, sometimes relationships break up with a lot of anger and resentment and one party may seek to hurt the other by destroying that person's beloved pet. In this case, the animal has been deprived from completing its mission with his or her person. When contacted in spirit form, the animal will express his or her sorrow and disappointment about what has occurred. I always ask the animal what happened upon their arrival in the afterlife. Consider the following story:

Buffy was a brown and white Jack Russell terrier living with a couple whose relationship was failing. On the day divorce papers were delivered to the husband, his anger soared. He decided to "punish" his wife in the most horrible way he could imagine and in his rage, went home and took their dog to the vet to be euthanized. When Buffy died, he was carried to the afterlife in the arms of a white angel with wings. When he arrived, Buffy was very angry and he showed me the angel talking to him about his feelings. He shared with me what the angel said to him which was something like, "Don't harbor any resentment about the circumstances of your death because it will keep new love from

Angel carrying an animal into the afterlife.

entering." Buffy said simply, *I spit it out!* Buffy was given what he termed a "rest life" in a home with two toddlers who loved him. He said it was like a vacation resort for toddlers! Buffy said the angels sent him there to learn how to be playful and happy again. According to Buffy, this would be a short life, and then he would come back to live with his person again.

How do you know when it is time to put an animal down?
Always ask the animal if it is ready. It is very important to be clear about whether an animal needs to be put down, or if its behavior is indicative of something else. Consider the following consultation:

A woman from New England called me to verify if her dog, Master, should be put down. Master stopped eating and drinking five days earlier and was so weak and dehydrated that he was no longer able to stand up for any length of time. I contacted Master, and the first impression that came through was that his "light" or life energy was still bright, indicating that he was not ready to depart. Along with the initial communication came the words, *The water's no good.* I related this to the woman, that is, that the dog was not ready to die and that he claimed the water had something wrong with it. I asked her what kind of water she had, city or well. She replied, "Well water." I asked the dog if he would drink something other than water. He said he would. I asked his person if she had any canned broth in the house, and would she open a can and offer it to Master. She did. The dog quickly drank the broth. I asked her to go to the market and buy some bottled water and offer it to Master, and then call me back. She gave him two gallons of bottled water, which she said Master drank and drank until it was all gone. I recommended that she have her well water tested. As it turned out, the well water sample contained E-coli, a dangerous bacterium which causes cholera. Master was trying to tell her by his behavior and body language, that the water was contaminated and she should not drink it. She was not aware of it, nor did she become sick, because she had other beverages to drink, including milk, soda, juice, soup, and other liquid refreshments. Master had only the water to drink, and became immediately aware that it didn't taste right, and that he felt "funny" after drinking it.

Life energy. When you communicate with an animal, you "see" the animal with inner vision (across the screen of your consciousness). You also see what I call the *life energy* in the form of light radiating from the animal. I classify this light on a scale from one to ten, with ten being the bright life energy light of a puppy or kitten. Compare it with a light that is on a dimmer switch. When the dimmer is on full, the animal has a full life ahead of him. As the animal ages, its light dims. On my scale, a light value of five means that the animal is in good health and is about half-way through his life span — for dogs about six to seven years old, for cats about seven to eight years old. If an animal appears as a two on the life energy scale, he is either very old or very sick. It becomes time to inquire about his chronological age and also about his health. When the animal's life energy reaches a one on the scale, I can barely make contact with him as he is fading out of his physical body. This is the time when I ask the animal if he is ready to be put down. The answer is always yes.

Saying "good bye." One of the hardest decisions is when to release your pet from suffering and put him down. Animals will telepathically send messages to you when their time is near. Also, the animal's person will begin to feel the beginnings of a detachment between himself and his pet. The person will then go to extreme measures and heroic attempts to extend the life of the animal. It has been my experience that the person always knows when it is time to let his pet go. People say good-bye in many different ways. Some people will have a family get-together to say good bye; others will cook a special dinner for the animal with all the corresponding treats. Often the person will wait until moments before the animal receives the injection and just say, "Good bye, I love you."

From the animal's perspective, the cycle of birth, life and death is a natural experience and should be treated as just that. The animal usually wants to tell his person how he feels and express his gratitude and affection before departing. For example, common farewells go something like this: *Thank you for taking me in and giving me a good home. I am grateful for all that you did in caring for me. I had a good time and appreciate all the love that you gave me. I love you too, and will never forget you.*

It makes no difference whether the animal is about to die or if he is being turned over to a shelter for adoption. If an animal is dropped off at a shelter, and the owner does not relate to the animal his reasons for giving him up, the animal will often feel rejected, wondering what he did wrong to cause his person to reject him. Simply talking to the animal in words, explaining the reason he is being placed in adoption, will save the animal feelings of guilt, shame, abandonment, and self-doubt. These feelings will carry over to any future relationship. A little simple kindness at the time of separation will help the animal to avoid separation pain.

Grieving. Separation is one of the most painful experiences in life. Emotionally, separating from someone or something very dear to you is about as bad an experience as life presents. Sometimes the loss of a pet can leave a painful hole in your heart that feels like the size of the Grand Canyon. Inconsolable sorrow can often have a positive effect on spiritual growth. The pain that won't go away can turn into a quest for answers on a spiritual level. For example, in my own case, the pain of losing my cat, Frosty, was more than I could bear. His death followed the death of my husband by only three months. The only way I could deal with the loss on a temporary basis was to promise myself that somehow, I would find a way to reconnect with them while I was still in the physical dimension. My search led to the discovery of animal telepathic communication.

Leaving the Body and the Transition.

I have spoken to hundreds of animals in the afterlife. I ask them to describe how they made the transition from the physical dimension to the spiritual one. About ninety percent of animals responded by describing the appearance of a white figure with wings that enters the room just prior to death. Animals say they are angels, and as I connect with them I can confirm what they are saying is accurate. The white angel, which looks transparent with light shining through it, very much like the sun's rays piercing through the clouds, always has large white wings. Some are male, some female — I think. I can't really tell the difference, except that some angels have very long white flowing hair that actually gets caught up in their wings. The angel picks up the animal's ethereal or spirit body, which looks like an apparition (you can see through it) and carries it to the afterlife. Sometimes the pet is welcomed to the afterlife by family members or other animals that he knew during his current incarnation.

The afterlife. Animals in spirit form show me where they are in the afterworld, and what other beings are present. About ninety percent go to a place that looks like a really clean and well-tended park area. There, dogs are playing about with children, chasing after Frisbees, sticks and balls, and there are children on swings. For cats, there is always a large fish pond about twenty feet wide and stocked with giant goldfish. The pond is shallow, about one foot deep, and the cats put their paws in the water to play with the fish but not kill them. I don't know why the remaining ten percent of animals who cross over do not show me the angel accompanying them there. It may have something to do with their particular person's belief systems. For example, if their person doesn't believe in reincarnation, or in angels, the animal will not answer my questions when I ask. Animals tell me that they never say anything that will be in conflict with their person's beliefs. Animals know at what level their persons are in terms of spiritual growth and never go beyond those boundaries.

Some animals go to a place where there appears to be only clouds. They are literally walking on clouds and air. Once I saw beings that had bright light radiating from them. Angels with wings surrounded the dog. I asked the dog who these light beings were. He answered, *Those are angels too. You have only seen angels with wings, but angels have other forms too.* Just then, a host of white angels the size of butterflies floated and flew around the dog. They were very graceful in their movements and reminded me of the ballet, *Swan Lake.* On another occasion, I had a consultation with a white Persian cat who was in the afterlife. She was also in the clouds and was surrounded by other white Persian cats that had light shining through them. The kitty was very busy and I asked her how she was doing. She answered, *I am busy making a place for my mommy when it is her turn to cross over.* Later, I discovered that her person loved Persian cats, and in her retirement started breeding Persians as both a hobby and for extra income. She always had about six white Persians in her home.

One particular consultation with an animal in the afterlife involved a dog in the baby realm of angels. Sugar was a blonde cocker spaniel who was very small for her breed, measuring about sixteen to eighteen inches long and standing only about ten inches high weighing about thirteen pounds when he got her, and filled out more later to about eighteen pounds. Her person, Gary Knox, called me to contact Sugar in spirit form. Sugar was a petite, charming little girl with the grace and poise of a princess. She had succumbed to cancer and Gary wanted to know if he had left any stones unturned in trying to save her. I asked Sugar about this, and she answered, *No, it was just my time to go.* I asked her to show me how she entered the afterlife.

A baby angel (cherub) *picked me up and we flew to this park.*

I saw the cherub as she held her arms around Sugar and carried her off. I asked her to show me where she was now. She showed me a scene in a park, and she was surrounded by infants and toddlers, as if she was reading them a story or reciting a poem.

"Why are you there?"

The cherub put me here because these babies and toddlers never had a pet. I am here to teach them the loving bond between babies and animals. Babies and animals have always been able to communicate with each other. These babies died before they had that chance.

It was one of the sweetest scenes I have ever had the privilege to witness.

Sometimes angels incarnate as animals in order to help a particular person during a very hard time in their life. These animals usually don't live very long lives, and are called back when they have finished their missions. For example, a colleague of mine owned two white poodles. One of them, Bow, died suddenly of a heart attack at age four years. He called me because his wife was so upset that he thought

Sugar

talking to me might help. While we were on the telephone, one of his toddler nieces came over and looked at the poodle's body lying on a pillow. She told her uncle that she saw Bow "Up in the air and that he had wings." I contacted Bow, and he explained that he was an angel who incarnated into Bow's body for a short time to help the family get adjusted to their new home. The family consisted of the wife and her four teenage children and the husband who had never become a father. Quite an adjustment, I thought. Bow told me that angels do not have to go into a deep sleep to regenerate their life energy like other animals do in the afterlife, because new life energy is always flowing through them from the universe, so they can be ready in an instant to help wherever they are needed.

The re-energizing and deep sleep. After animals spend a few weeks or months (in our time) in the afterlife getting used to existing in an etheric body and learning how to move about in the afterlife, they go into a deep sleep for several weeks, months, or years. During this time, they undergo a regeneration process which involves the restoration of life energy. One can think of it as sort of "recharging their batteries." During this time, it is very hard to communicate with them, but not impossible. After an animal has been recharged with life energy, its form will change. It appears once again as almost solid, that is, in its physical form. At that time, the animal is permitted to choose what he would like to do for his next life. It may want to stay in the spirit world to work with several animal councils that exist there. The councils' purpose is to find ways to enlighten humans and also other animals about their species, so it does not become extinct. According to some animals, the afterlife offers a number of "schools" for animals to attend and learn more about diverse forms of life. If animals want to come back to the physical dimension, they begin to look around for a new body to enter. Picking a new body is solely their decision. They can come back as anything they want to experience — an animal, a plant, a rock, and yes, even a human. Animals tell me that humans are afforded the same options by All That Is (the Creator). They are permitted any life experience they desire.

Reincarnation: The return. Animals go from life to life as easily as we breathe, and unlike humans, remember their past lives. Animals are consciously aware of their immortality. I asked animals why humans don't remember their own past lives.

Humans choose not to remember their past lives because it increases the intensity of the adventure of the new life they are about to begin.

When an animal reincarnates, it is the same soul (or spirit), but in a different body. Most of the personality and characteristics remain. If the breed or species is dramatically different, then genetics plays an important part of the new personality.

Reincarnated animals remember their homes, where the litter box is kept, and their favorite places to hide or sleep. They remember the other pets in the home, and the other pets recognize them as well. Some memories return slowly, because the soul has entered a baby body once more. Some behaviors have to be re-trained, and this is especially true for dogs.

Appointment to a person. Once animals decide to return, they are appointed to their person. I have asked hundreds of animals, "Who does the appointing?" and they will not give me an answer. I don't know if it is the angels, God, a keeper of souls or something else, or if they are just not permitted to say. They just don't give me an answer at all. However, once they are appointed to their person, there is nothing that can stand in the way of animals uniting with their person. Consider the following:

Miss Wings' Story.

I was invited again by Mary Ellen Angelscribe and Maureen McCullough to be a guest on "Angel Waves" radio show on WSAI in Cincinnati. A few months later, Mary Ellen phoned and asked about her cat, Camalot, who is in the spirit world. Camalot was happy and anxious to communicate. *Tell Mommy I am fine. I have been renewed with life energy and I want to come back as a kitten and live with her some more.*

Camalot showed me an image of the body he would be incarnated into: a Silver Shaded Persian, female. He said he would be born sometime in December and would be ready to come home in late January or February.

Mary Ellen was concerned about the cost of the Silver Shaded Persian because of recent medical bills. I asked Camalot about this.

Don't worry, Mommy, I have been assigned to you and nothing can stop that once it is predestined. You don't need money, only faith that I will be yours.

I assured Mary Ellen that Camalot was right. Once an animal is appointed to you, nothing can touch them or stand in their way.

Mary Ellen started combing the local shelters and newspapers and finally, the Internet for the kitten. She came upon Linda LeColst, a breeder of Shaded Silver Persians in Boston. One of her cats, Ballerina, had a kitten on December 8 and, a few days later, Linda noticed that her tail wasn't just right. A few weeks later, Linda took two of her kittens to be photographed. One of the photographer's props that were available was a pair of angel wings. The photographer put the wings on the tailless kitten and thought, "Hmmm, I wonder if the injured kitten belongs to Mary Ellen."

Linda was concerned about giving the injured kitten a good home, so near the end of December, Linda wrote to Mary Ellen about giving the kitten to her as a special gift. Linda doesn't ship her kittens. The new owner/person has to come and pick it up.

That's when the miracle took place, and many people from the airlines and other places came forward and offered to escort the kitten from Boston to Oregon for free. All went well, and a woman named Vivian Rozane of Maryland escorted the kitten. When the kitten, who she named, "Miss Wings," arrived in Oregon, Mary Ellen called me for another consultation.

Miss Wings said, *I told you, Mommy, you didn't need money, only faith to bring us together. All the time I was in the airplane a lady angel with long white hair was with me to keep me from being scared. When the lady Vivian gave me to you, the angel said good-bye and left.*

I asked Miss Wings what her mission in this life was.

My mission is to teach that miracles happen.

Miss Wings sent me an image of the angel. She looked like a pure white apparition, with long, flowing white hair that covered her shoulders and part of her wings as well.

There were three angels in that airplane that day, Miss Wings, the angel from Heaven, and Vivian.

I must admit that I know very little about angels and had not "seen" one until the animals showed me their transition to

Miss Wings taking a rest after flight.

the afterlife. There are, however, those who are experts on angels including Mary Ellen Angelscribe, and Dr. Doreen Virtue[5]. The reader is referred to these two sources for more information on the subject.

Walk-ins.

A number of years ago Washington columnist and writer Ruth Montgomery wrote a book called *Strangers Among Us*[6], describing a phenomenon she termed walk-ins. These were supposedly enlightened beings who wanted to enter the physical dimension for a time to accomplish a specific mission, but without the usual process of birth, growing up, and reschooling. According to Montgomery, the entry of a spirit into an existing physical body occupied by someone else required a contractual agreement between the person in physical form and the spirit entity. A person in physical form who wished to depart, or could no longer face the challenges or problems of life, has the opportunity to leave and re-enter the spiritual domain without the usual penalties associated with suicide. The contract included the entering spirit agreeing to complete the life mission of the departing spirit. Because the entering spirit is not emotionally entangled in the departing spirit's control dramas, it is easy to accomplish his mission within a short time. There occur several "trial periods" in which the spirits can exchange places for a time to sort of test the waters, so to speak. If mutually agreed, then the departing spirit will leave and the entering spirit will take over the physical body permanently.

Montgomery interviewed many walk-ins and found similar circumstantial changes evident in their behaviors which wreaked havoc on the departing person's family and friends. Almost always, the person who now occupied the body of the departed spirit, was so different in personality, that the spouses felt like they were strangers. Many couples divorced because of it. Much to my surprise, some of these walk-ins appeared on national television to tell their stories.

I have encountered in my telepathic communications with animals four such entities. One was a wolf, one a horse, and the other two dogs. For example, the wolf was my friend Becky's pet Dusty that died of cancer four years earlier. I spoke with Dusty prior to her death and also in spirit form several times and was familiar with her particular energy. Some time later, Becky rescued another wolf/coyote mix and brought her home to join her family. As I spoke with the wolf, which she named Cassie, something inside me saw a bond of love with my friend that was very intense, that I somehow recognized. I said to Becky, "I may be wrong, but I think this animal is your wolf Dusty reincarnated." She said it couldn't be, because Dusty said she was not coming back. I insisted that the rescued wolf was Dusty. She called another animal communicator who confirmed that the rescued wolf was indeed Dusty.

Dusty told me that the wolf/part coyote body she entered was cold, hungry, and was suffering from heart worms and wanted to depart. Just at that time, Becky was experiencing health problems. Dusty wanted to come back to give her healing energy. I asked Dusty how she came back and did she need permission from the angels to do so?

My Mommy called me back with her heart. You don't need permission from anyone to come back to your family. It doesn't matter if it is for her benefit or my own.

Dusty, can I ask you another question?
Sure.

When you entered this new body of Cassie, how did it feel?
Wimpy!

She made me burst out laughing until my sides were splitting. Dusty was pure wolf and Cassie was a wolf/coyote mix.

A door opens. My second encounter with a walk-in occurred when another dear friend, Rose, found a stray and wanted to adopt him. She said the dog wouldn't go up the stairs, or pass through any doorways and asked me if I would talk to him for her. The dog said he was not ready to communicate with me. I sensed from his energy, that he was her former dog, Starlight, whom I had communicated with a few times in the spirit world. I was ninety-five percent sure that the stray was Starlight, but I told the friend that unless I confirmed that with the dog, I couldn't be positive. One week later, I returned to the house. The dog confirmed that he was Starlight, and that he was a walk-in. He wanted to return to help Rose, who was ill, but he knew that she was in no position to adopt a puppy and go through the rigors of training. Starlight saw a young dog that had been abandoned in an empty parking lot on a snowy evening. That night, Rose's roommate, Katy, was driving, and noticed the dog shivering in the snow. She picked him up and turned him over to the dog warden at the local police department. When she returned home, she told Rose about the dog and the next morning she went to investigate. Both women said they were strangely drawn to the dog, and decided to take him home on a trial basis for adoption.

I knew that the dog was a walk-in and asked him to show me how this occurred. He showed me the scene of Katy driving and spotting the dog shivering. Just then, a "door" opened from another dimension. It looked like it was about eight feet high and four feet wide and there was a light coming from behind the opening. The opening was about five to seven feet above ground level. There stood the spirit of Starlight beside an angel. From the dog's perspective in the spirit world, and looking into the physical dimension, our world looked like a videotape being played on fast forward and in black and white. As the roommate came near, the angel said, "Now," and Starlight jumped into the dog's body. After Katy dropped him off with the police, a door opened again and he was called back into the spirit world.

The next day, when Rose went to see him, the same thing happened. The moment she entered the police station, the door to the spiritual dimension opened again, and there stood Starlight with the angel. Again, the angel said, "Now," and Starlight jumped into the dog's body. I asked Starlight why he was afraid of the stairs and doorways.

I was not fully assimilated into this body, because I didn't know if Rose and Katy would adopt me. Every time I looked at a doorway, I thought I was being asked to come back to the spirit dimension and became very confused.

The view from above. When I returned home, I connected with Becky's wolf Dusty in spirit. I asked him to describe to me what this dimension (the physical dimension) looked like from the afterlife.

I am looking right now into my mom's living room. Everything looks the same as it did in my physical body. The furniture looks the same, my mom looks the same, and you look the same, he answered.

"Is it in 3 dimensions, and is it color or black and white?"

Of course, it's in 3 dimensions – it looks THE SAME, and it is in color.

"What was I seeing in black and white like a videotape when I talked with Starlight?"

Oh! What you saw was the entire life story of the abandoned dog, so that when Starlight entered his body he would have some memory of the prior experiences of that body up to that time. A spirit cannot just enter a life at any time, because it would be like just being born that minute. The angel showed Starlight the portion of the dog's life story he would need to remember or know about when he entered the physical body of the dog and the physical dimension.

"Dusty, I have an important question to ask you. Is the entire life story of every being already written somewhere, even if it hasn't been lived yet?"

Yes, but it is like a long string, and at any point along the string are many different paths and outcomes.

Dusty showed me an image of a string with frays that contain many smaller strings within it (something like fiber optic cable).

These are many different possible outcomes the being may choose during the course of his lifetime.

"Does that mean that the future is already written and we are all just pawns in the game?"

No, it just means that all the possibilities and outcomes are already available and accounted for.

"Who makes all these possibilities?"

Your own spirit does.

Horse Trader. My encounter with a horse proved to be especially enlightening. Jill Gabel called me about her horse Trader who had just passed away. Trader was a beautiful Sorrel (dark red) horse with a white star on his forehead. He was fifteen years old, and had arthritis in his legs. A farrier tried to correct the situation by trimming Traders' hoofs into a new "natural" trim which mean shearing off the soles of his hooves to the ground so he would not "break over" at the knees because of his arthritis. Instead, the trim caused him to abscess in the hooves and consequently foundered complete with bone rotation through the soles of his hooves. Within days, Trader was unable to stand and became crippled and subsequently died. Jill was heartbroken and prayed to the universe pleading for Trader to come back to her. As she left the barn, she came upon a single white feather, which she picked up and saved.

A week later, Jill came upon a horse for adoption named Dakota, who belonged to her friend. Jill was in no mood to adopt another horse, because she was still grieving for Trader. As she looked at Dakota, something in his eyes caught her attention, and her heart was strangely warmed. Something told her to adopt Dakota so she took him home. Dakota gave her no trouble getting into the trailer, and seemed to know where his paddock was. He went over to the place where Jill had buried Trader and began to roll over and over on the grave. Jill noticed that Dakota was behaving in the same manner as Trader did and even ate his carrots in the same way.

Jill called me for a consultation. I connected with Trader in spirit, and he quickly showed me his etheric body and then showed me the body of a beautiful brown horse about the same age, which I described to Jill. "That's Dakota!" she said. As I connected with Dakota, I recognized his energy to be that of Trader. I asked Trader/Dakota how this came about. He told me that he was not supposed to die this early in his life, because he had not completed his mission with Jill. When Jill pleaded with the universe for him to come back to her, he showed me that an angel — who was the mythical winged horse, Pegasus — came to get him and take him into the afterlife. Pegasus took a feather from his wing and dropped it on the hay on the floor of the stable. Trader entered the spirit world. During this same time, Dakota's owner decided to reduce the number of horses she owned, and to offer Dakota for adoption. Dakota didn't want to belong to someone else and wanted to depart his body. On the day that Jill came, Trader showed me a large opening appeared between this dimension and the afterlife. It rested on the ground and was about the size of a barn door. There stood Trader with an Angel (a female) with long white hair. As Jill approached Dakota, the Angel said "Now" and Trader's spirit entered the body of Dakota. Dakota walked through the door and he and the Angel disappeared behind it.

Trader's story touched me deeply, and this was the second time that I have been witness to Pegasus. It is a very humbling experience to see and communicate with him, and I was deeply honored to see him again. Pegasus must exist in an angelic realm, I thought, because his physical appearance was white and transparent and that would explain the wings. Trader said he was not meant to die at this time. He related to me that his return was brought about by Jill's heart and also by his own, so he could complete his mission with Jill. He explained that he and Jill were meant to be together because Jill understood the mystical union of horse and rider. Jill's path included using her ability to view everything from a unity perspective. When I told this to Jill, she said, "Yes, I know what you mean, I see everything in existence as part of the one life, all connected by love."

Angels appear to play a major role in the transition of animals from one dimension to another. Once I became used to seeing them in spirit form among animals and assisting them in one way or another, it became almost second nature to see angels and animals together. I have tried to listen to what the angels say to the animals, but all I can get is what the animal is hearing the angel say. I cannot hear the angel's communications directly because angels exist on a higher spiritual level. I am always astounded by the extent the universe will go to bring loved ones back into our lives.

CHAPTER TEN

The Animal Consultation Process

Animal Communicators.

People who communicate with animals on a professional level are among the nicest people on Earth. It is my experience that students who attend animal communication workshops are different from most other people. By this I mean, that among their qualities, two traits stand out above the rest. First, they are loving and sincere in their interest in animals, and second, they are humble and unpretentious. Sincerity, intention, and openness to a new way of connecting with animals are paramount to developing good communication skills. Conducting workshops is a pleasure and an uplifting experience for everyone including the teacher. An introductory workshop usually consists of the basics of sending and receiving a communication from an animal. An advanced workshop consists of in-depth communications and interviewing skills.

What separates a great animal communicator from a fair one is that the former has great interviewing skills. Knowing the right questions to ask makes all the difference in the world. When communicating with an animal or other being, conversations can go on and on. But when the communicator is talking with a client, the communication has to be professional, focused, to the point, problems identified, and solutions found — all in a twenty- or thirty-minute period, because the client is paying for consultation time. Not an easy task! With practice, the telepath learns to focus in on the main purpose for the consultation first while leaving less threatening issues or questions for later.

What professional communicators bring into the consultation includes their knowledge, experiences, and compassion for both the client and the animal. When an impression or communication is received by telepaths, it must filter up through their brain and then become translated into language so it can be verbally expressed to the client. Thus, the more knowledge and experience the telepath has, the more detailed will be the answers. For example, if an animal is asked, "Are you in any pain or discomfort?" the answers will range from, *I have an upset tummy* to *There is an ulcer in the duodenum which is causing me pain.* The suffering animal will send a picture to the telepath of the alimentary tract indicating the size and location of the lesion.

The role of the client. In the interest of quality and economy, it is helpful if the client prepares questions for the pet ahead of time. Clients are often surprised by their pet's answers, because clients may have preconceived notions concerning what their pet thinks or feels. Animals are very concerned about their persons and know a great deal about their goals, aspirations, intentions, beliefs and feelings. Pets have a way of sending telepathic thoughts or ideas to their person which can help them to achieve their life purposes. Likewise, pets can withhold information which is likely to upset their persons, go against their belief systems, or cause them to harm another.

Once a communication begins, it takes its own form. The conversation between the animal and its person may or may not include input from the telepath. Some animal communicators do not become involved in the conversation at all. They simply relate the question to the pet and the pet's answer back to the client, without translation or interpretation. They don't initiate anything. They are much like the TTY operators for the deaf. They let the client and the pet do all the talking. Others, like me, give more detailed translations, especially if the communication involves the health or welfare of the animal. A client may be interested in communicating with an animal because it shows signs of illness but the veterinarian can find nothing wrong. Inquiry with the animal often reveals health problems that are difficult to detect during a routine physical examination. Among these might be the presence and location of small tumors, inflammatory conditions in the gastrointestinal tract, the presence of arthritis, or evidence of neurological disorders including stroke. Many dogs present with pain in the lumbar spine caused by a subluxation (a partial dislocation) of the spinal vertebra. In this case, the background and experience of the telepath in working with animals plays an important part in discovery of the problem. Also, the telepath often acts as a negotiator between what the client wants or expects from the pet, and how much the pet is able or willing to comply.

Counseling. My experience as a psychologist enters the communication process often as I assume the role of counselor. Counseling animals and their persons is not unlike doing psychotherapy. Some of the same principles apply. For example, a main goal is to open up communication and understanding between the client and the pet. Sometimes this requires looking into the background of the pet for the etiology of certain behavioral problems associated with attachment and loss and previous mistreatment of an animal prior to adoption in the current family. In animals adopted from shelters, often the pet is removed from the home without any explanation as to why the animal is being given to a shelter. This leaves the animal wondering what he did wrong to be punished in this way, without the opportunity to change the behavior that caused the separation. Counseling will reveal the source of the pet's sadness and often what is required is a simple explanation that the family couldn't keep him any longer because they were moving, getting divorced, and so on. Sadness and depression enter the picture because the animal was never afforded the opportunity to say "good bye" to the family, especially the children. The counselor is able to "see" what attachments the pet has, and if any of these are former family members. In this case, since the telepath is connected directly with the animal and the animal is connected with the prior family, it is possible through the telepath for the animal to say "good bye" to them. The animal is released from the past, and is now able to be fully present in its new family.

Problems with prior physical abuse can be treated in the same way. As the communicator queries the pet, it becomes apparent that the animal has been beaten or otherwise mistreated. By connecting with the animal, it becomes possible to also see what the perpetrator looked like and help the animal to release its fears. Animals do not seek revenge, nor do they harbor grudges.

Sometimes, all it takes is to have the animal thank the person for giving them a home and feeding them and then to say "good bye." Although this does in no way undo the mistreatment, most animals are willing to let go of the past - simply because they prefer to live in the present moment. For them, a bad experience becomes just another experience, without judgment or appraisal.

Fees. Most animal communicators have comparable fees. The communicator must enter an altered state to connect with the animal, and fees are based upon the amount of time spent in that state. Most consultations last about twenty to thirty minutes. If clients have many pets they wish to communicate with, it will take longer, even up to ninety minutes. In this case, clients are usually charged for every fifteen-minute segment, or by each minute.

Factors which affect the telepath and communication. It is difficult for the animal communicator to stay in the altered state for long periods. Telepathic communication requires a lot of mental energy to inhibit an individual's random thoughts and have a quiet mind to be an open listener to the animal. Rest periods are required between consultations for the communicator. Sometimes telepaths will experience difficulty in reaching the altered state by events in their own lives. Factors which affect the telepath's ability to enter and stay in the altered state include fatigue, emotional upset, pain, and pain-relieving medications. With fatigue, telepaths do not have the mental energy to inhibit their random thoughts from entering their quiet state of mind. With physical pain or emotional upset, the body's arousal system puts the mind on alert, and does not allow for a quiet meditative state. With pain medications, the central nervous system is dulled, and the telepath will have difficulty maintaining a meditative state due to low mental energy. It is the ethical responsibility of telepaths to inform the client when they are not feeling well enough to make a good connection with their pet and to ask the client to reschedule. The client will respect this and be thankful for the courtesy and honesty of the telepath.

The Process of Inquiry.

Consultations usually begin by ordinary conversation with the client to define the purpose of the call. Common beginning questions:

- What animal do you wish to communicate with today?
- Will you describe for me the age, sex, breed, and physical appearance of the animal?
- Tell me what is going on with (pet's name)? The client describes the presenting problem.
- Has the animal been seen by a veterinarian? What were his findings?
- When did this problem begin?

After the initial questions, the telepath opens a conversation with the animal to clarify the issues and problems. When each issue is discussed (e.g., cats not using the litter box or dogs biting) the communicator will relate the pet's answer to the client. If the problem is behavioral, it may be necessary to negotiate a solution between the animal and its person. If the purpose of the communication is health-related, the communicator will ask the pet to give details about the location and severity of the pain or discomfort. For me, it is helpful to have the animal send me a three-dimensional image of the inside of its body. It appears like an x-ray, with images of abnormalities and their location. Sometimes the animal will know what caused the pain or will be able to tell when it began. During this type of interview, the pet and communicator do most of the talking. Animals often know what they need to alleviate the problem and will ask for it specifically. For example, *I have a big hairball. Can you ask my mom to give me some of that stuff that tastes like caramel?*

Common Problems Addressed.

The two most common problems concern dogs biting or cats urinating outside the litter box.

In most cases, dogs bite because they are in some kind of pain. Dogs do not attack other beings because they don't like them. That would require a value judgment, which animals don't make. Sometimes, especially in small dogs, it is because of fear of attack by a larger animal or person, a matter of self-defense. Some owners train their dogs to be protection dogs, but then complain when the dog protects them by biting persons who are invited into their homes. When training a protection dog, it is necessary to clearly define who and what the dog is supposed to protect the family from. Consultations with protection dogs will usually involve explaining to the animal that persons who come into the house are invited, and the dog is not allowed to attack them. Persons outside the house (or the perimeter of the property) are not invited and the dog is allowed to bark or otherwise chase them away. The dog can't sort out who is friend or foe unless the owner states it beforehand. If the problem is the dog barking at the mailman every day, it can be easily solved by explaining to the dog that the mailman is outside the house and is to be left alone. Dogs usually respond to simple definitions like this.

Cats are a different story. Cats are hard-wired to protect a family within a certain area, usually the inside of the house. Cats have the ability to lay down an energy grid to include all objects within the house. This takes a lot of mental energy for the cat and the energy has to be maintained even when the cat is asleep. If something is moved, added, or otherwise disturbs the energy grid, the animal must draw back the grid, reconsolidate, and lay it back down again. This process takes about three days and requires a great deal of mental energy. During this time, the boundaries are unprotected and the cat responds by leaving its scent, which is a much stronger marker. To avoid this, it is helpful for the owner/person to tell the cat in advance what he/she is planning to do. The cat then can open the grid to allow for the change. Believe it or not, this works every time!

Feral Animals.

All animals have missions to fulfill during their sojourn on the Earth. As much as humans feel compassion regarding feral animals, many of them chose to be in this kind of environment prior to their incarnation. Not all animals, especially cats, want to be rescued. I have had many conversations with stray and feral cats who tell me that their mission is predatory, and that their job is to keep the rat/mouse population at bay. Some animals choose to roam the streets in the wild so that homeless and other indigent people can have the experience of unconditional love without the responsibility of a personal pet and its accompanying expenses. Some cats tell me that they choose to roam park-like areas where children congregate to provide unconditional love experiences to children whose parents won't allow pets in their homes for various reasons. I have communicated with many lost cats who tell me that they were born to be feral cats and ran away from home to fulfill their missions. The owner is often dismayed at why a cat would leave a warm, loving home with abundant food to return to a life in the wild where its well-being is tenuous. The universe provides for all life forms in many different ways. Many times, animals will choose their missions according to the needs of the greater community, and not only for the needs of single individuals or families. The life choices of the animals must be respected in the same manner as desires and choices of individual persons.

Consultations With Animals.

All consultations with animals are interesting and uplifting for the client, the animal, and the communicator. However, some consultations are so profound that they take people into unexplored territories and new realms. A few of these incidences are included in other chapters; others are included here.

Inner vision. A woman from the Arizona Humane Society called me about a dog I will call Buddy that was found tied to a tree in the mountains. When dropped off at the shelter, it was apparent that the dog's eyes were gouged out and it was blind. Buddy must have been blind for some time, because the surrounding tissue was completely healed. The woman from the shelter adopted the dog and had him for about two years when she heard about me and called. I spoke with Buddy, who did not seem to be in distress. Buddy told me that he once belonged to a boy about ten years old with cerebral palsy. The boy (in a wheelchair) was permitted to bring the dog to school with him for protection and companionship. A few boys in his classroom and another older boy were jealous of the boy's relationship with the dog, and one day took the dog into the woods and gouged out his eyes with a pocket knife. Someone found the dog and took it to the vet for medical care. The boy still wanted to keep Buddy because being a handicapped person himself, he did not view the dog as being anything less than a whole being. Some time later, the boy passed away. The father, who was a believer in nature's way of balancing things, left the dog tied to the tree as prey for the local mountain lions.

What astounded and fascinated me about this story was that the dog, Buddy, had learned to navigate by using inner vision alone. When I communicated with Buddy, he told me how he managed to get around. I asked him to show me what he sees. He sent me slightly blurred images of his surroundings, which were clear enough to navigate. Buddy said that the boy had become his "eyes" in the aftermath of the incident and that he could see primarily through inner vision accomplished telepathically between him and the boy. When the boy died, Buddy had trouble navigating without the boy's help and the father took him to the woods to die.

The Humane Society took the dog in and one of the veterinary technicians adopted him. In his new home, she noticed that he could navigate very well without eyes. Another one of her dogs, Little Gal, befriended Buddy and communicated her vision telepathically to the dog in the same manner as did the boy, always looking out for staircases, furniture in the way, and so on. Buddy's feelings about himself and his relationship to other dogs and humans were not different than any other animal I have communicated with. Buddy saw himself as a whole being, just living his life in love and companionship with others. He ate, slept and played the same as any pet in the family, requiring no special treatments for his special needs. The best part is that he harbored no resentment towards his attackers. A remarkable animal indeed!

The phenomenon of telepathy being used to provide sensory information from one being to another has only been referred to in mystical literature. It is the ability to see, hear, taste, or smell without the usual sense organs. Some sages and enlightened teachers claim to have the ability to see through their ears, and hear through their skin, and other fantastic phenomena. These teachers claim that the universe contains all information, and that within each photon of light or the smallest unit of energy, the entire universe is contained in its entirety. To observe, one merely needs to pay attention. In my communications with Buddy, I was reminded of an example of this phenomenon that was presented in the TV series Kung Fu. The master was blind, but could identify the student "grasshopper" and distinguish him from all other life forms or objects by paying attention to all that was around him. In other words, experience life — all life. Like Merlin, in his teachings to the young King Arthur, he instructed his student, "If you want to think like a bird, become birds."

Maya's moving. A woman called me from Cleveland to consult with her five cats. One cat, Maya, developed a problem urinating inappropriately in corners of the house and in her nervousness, licked a great deal of her hair off her body so she was actually bald in spots. During the initial conversation with her person, I discovered that the lady's house was up for sale, because her job was transferred to another city. Maya was a stray cat who found a new home and family with the lady. Maya's distress started when prospective buyers (strangers) began coming in and out of the house on a daily basis. Maya believed it was her responsibility to put her energy field around everyone who entered her energy field space, and was mentally exhausted expending all the energy that required. She began to feel irritated, saw herself as a failure, and her skin became dry and itchy, forming "hot spots" which she licked and licked to moisten. Her person was unaware that Maya experienced the same situation in her previous family, who moved away leaving Maya behind to fend for herself. The lady reassured Maya that she would not be left behind again. I explained to Maya that the persons coming in and out of the house were just visitors looking to see if they were interested in buying the house and that Maya had no responsibility towards them whatsoever. This lifted a great burden from Maya's shoulders and her nervous condition went away. She moved to the new home without any problem.

Never underestimate the dedication an animal has to its job or mission. In Maya's case, she was willing to undergo extreme stress in her attempts to protect the members of the home with her energy. She needed only to have her person define who family was and who was not.

Fear of flying. A couple called me from Tennessee about their three-year-old Newfoundland dog, Newfie. Newfie had severe allergies since he came to them at eight weeks of age. They had spent a fortune going from specialist to specialist to relieve the dog's itching, hot spots, and skin and ear infections. He barked and trembled when seeing other dogs and strangers, and anything that was new. When I spoke to Newfie, I discovered the origin of his nervousness. The couple purchased him from a breeder in Kansas, and had him flown to Tennessee so they could pick him up. Newfie showed me that he was deadly afraid of the darkness of the luggage bay area where he was kept, the sound of the engines, and the tilting of the plane during take-off and landing. For him, he was in the most terrifying situation of his life and he wanted his mother. I helped Newfie overcome his fears by taking him, in his mind, back to the time he boarded the plane. Each step of the journey, he related to me what he was hearing and feeling. As he did this, I reminded him that what he wasn't remembering was that he was okay, not injured, and was still alive. At each step of the process, I added the memory that he was okay, and that he is still okay now. After Newfie finished telling me his horror story, he felt a lot better. I assured him that this was only one bad experience in his life that would never happen again. I told Newfie that his new mom and dad would tell him (in words) if they were going someplace new and explain what would be there, and what to expect, which they were glad to do. Newfie's allergies subsided considerably. He is off most of his medications and has placed his love and trust in the hands of his persons.

Victim behavior. Some animals actually attract aggressive attacks by other animals. These animals exhibit what is called victim behavior. An animal sitting in a crouched posture hissing or growling will incite another animal to attack by virtue that the animal's behavior may be perceived as an impending attack upon him. Squirt is one such cat.

Squirt was one among five kittens born into a loving family that included three adult cats — one her father and one her mother. Squirt was an outgoing, happy and precocious kitten and was adopted by a young man in his twenties. The man loved her, but worked two jobs and Squirt was left alone most of the time. About six months later, the gentleman moved to an apartment complex that did not allow pets. He brought Squirt back to her previous home, where she was accepted back into the fold. However, Squirt was unfamiliar with the other cats in the house, even her own mother and hid in the corner most of the time hissing at any cat (or person) who walked by. She finally isolated herself from the other cats by jumping up on the kitchen counter and cabinets, where she took up residence during the day. At night, she would come down and explore the house and return to her "nest in the sky" during the day. Her owner contacted me because Squirt began to urinate on top of the cabinet. Squirt related to me her fears. Although she was born into a gregarious family, she lived most of her developmental months with only a single person, who was rarely there to interact with her. Squirt is like many animals that have the ability to connect with only one person or animal. Everything is on a one-to-one basis — almost symbiotic in nature, but without the clinging. Squirt's person was disappointed because she wanted to hold and pet the cat, but Squirt wouldn't hear of it. We finally reached an agreement, whereby the person would hang her arm over the side of the bed and Squirt would rub up against the arm for a few minutes each day. The lady moved to a new house with a glass-enclosed sunroom. Squirt's toys, food and litter box were moved to the sunroom and it became her safe-haven, where she could take her time to observe the behavior of the other cats without having physical contact. After awhile, her familiarity with the other cats allowed her to come out and interact with them without fear.

When animals exhibit victim or similar behaviors, it is natural for members of the pack or colony to attack them. In the wild, they do this so that the "weak" one is not found by predators that often will attack the entire group. This behavior can be seen following visits to the vet. Upon returning home, the family pets hiss or growl at the animal. In most cases, the family animals smell something different about the pet — usually alcohol from a shot. To stop this, I recommend that the person take an alcohol swab and wipe it on all the animals in the house so they all smell the same way.

Words of love from beyond. Tyler was a champion greyhound adopted by Anita Vlchek at Tyler's retirement from racing. Like many greyhounds that race, Tyler developed some abnormal bone tissue on his front and back legs. In addition, later in his life, Tyler began having epileptic seizures. Sometimes epileptic activity arises from small lesions in the brain due to excess physical activity (in this case racing) increasing blood pressure and causing small blood vessels to rupture.

Tyler related to me that his mission was to inspire people to be the best they can be. He loved racing and the attention he received for his performances. He was a true champion. Successful, but humble. Later, Tyler passed away. After he died, Tyler telepathically sent a poem to Anita's husband. With permission from Anita, I am enclosing a letter that she sent me regarding Tyler, his mission, and the poem.

Tyler

Dear Dr. Thomas,

I've been thinking a lot about Tyler's mission. To inspire people to be the best they can be. He certainly did that for me. We battled his seizures together for three years. I never let them bother me because they didn't keep him down. And I never gave up the fight and continued for three years to look for better ways to control them. I viewed it as a challenge. It was me against the seizures. On my Internet canine epilepsy discussion list, it is always me who is the party pooper. When everyone else wants to whine about what a horrible disease epilepsy is and how much their dogs suffer every day, I get on there and tell them my point of view. I never believed that Tyler suffered, either during his seizures or between them. (*This is true! Animals are not aware of their seizures.* Italics mine.) And I always tell them that attitude is everything. If you keep an optimistic attitude, your dog will also be happy and optimistic.

I sometimes forget myself and let things get to me and bring me down. From now on I will remember Tyler's mission and maybe I won't forget myself so often.

Thank you from the bottom of my heart,

Anita

P.S. I have enclosed the poem that I believe Tyler sent to my husband. When I told him what I had found out in talking to Tyler, he told me that this incident actually happened at Halloween last year. The music that is referred to is from the sound track of the IMAX movie, *The Living Sea* written by Sting. The particular song my husband was listening to at the time these words came to him is called "Why Should I Cry For You?"

LISTEN TO THE MUSIC
By Tyler

Listen to this music and think of me. Especially starting with cut number two, turn down the lights and close your eyes. Sit back and imagine me running.
I'm running free.
See me running? Just for the joy of it.
I'm doing what was meant to be.
In a field or on a track.
I'm running, running, running free.
I'm running free of leash or collars,
With the music, can you see?
I'm coming around the final turn,
See me run, I'm running free.
No more medicine or pills,
I'm running free of pain.
My legs are fluid, free of stiffness,
I run in sun or rain.
No racing silks or post time bets,
No more car rides to the vet's,
Because now I'm running happily,

Can you see I'm running free?
In slow motion or full speed ahead,
As you listen, imagine me,
It really isn't difficult,
Because I'm running, running free.

Where would I be without you?

Tyler

PART THREE
CHAPTER ELEVEN

Telepathy: How It Really Works

Humans already have the ability to communicate telepathically with animals simply because humans are members of the animal kingdom. It is natural, not supernatural. The human brain is innately hard-wired for telepathic communication. It is the ancient way of communicating with others. Telepathy is mainly a right-brain function. The right side of the brain is responsible for holistic concepts and putting things together. The left side of the brain is analytical and primarily used for language. The telepathic skills humans possessed in ancient times are still present, but have been neglected. This skill can be restored today. All it takes is a little knowledge about how it works and learning how to listen.

Webster's Collegiate Dictionary defines telepathy as "the transfer of thought from one being to another through extrasensory perception." What is being transferred is an impression of everything a particular being sees, hears, tastes, smells, and touches at any given moment in time. Researchers like Michael Talbot[1] describe it as a "thought ball," because of its completeness and detail. This impression is decoded by the brain and then translated into language. Where does it reside in the brain? It resides within the realm of imagination. That does not mean that it is imaginary. The word "imagine" comes from the Greek word, "imago," meaning to create a "likeness or duplicate" in the mind. This likeness is projected across the screen of one's consciousness. Mystics call the screen of consciousness the "third eye," or "inner vision." It is really a form of intuition. It is "a knowing" about something without the usual physical evidence to prove it within the environmental milieu. Telepathic communication with animals is not mind-to-mind communication as it is generally thought. It is spirit-to-spirit communication brought about by tapping into the universal mind. If it were brain-to-brain communication, then how would it be possible to communicate with a disembodied spirit in the afterlife that has no brain?

Where is the Mind?

There is a growing body of evidence that suggest the mind is not a faculty of the brain but of the spirit. Medical science assumed that the mind and brain were one. This was based upon clinical findings in patients with head or brain injuries and disease. Following trauma to the brain, the patient was reported to lose some or all brain function, which expressed itself in a variety of ways. Deepak Chopra[2 - 3] has suggested the brain is really a decoder of energy and information from the universe. The witness or observer is outside the brain and contained within the realm of spirit. In Chopra's model, the observer, the process of observation, and the observed are one. One can think of spirit as the human energy field described by Valerie Hunt[4]. We can

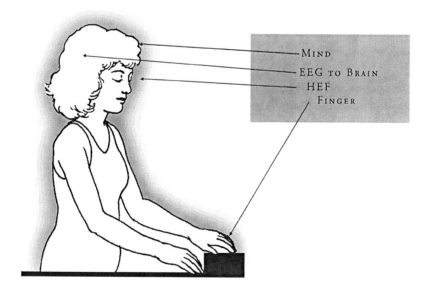

MIND
EEG TO BRAIN
HEF
FINGER

measure it, record from it, and notice variation in thought and how that thought affects the aura. There are computer programs available by which a special camera is able to detect the HEF in all its varied colors and project it onto the computer screen. As the person varies his thoughts, his aura or HEF will change in both color and intensity. The more esoteric the thought, the more the colors violet and white appear. Thoughts of compassion and healing bring about green and blue changes. Thoughts of the Divine bring about the colors violet and white, often with long white spikes emanating from the aura around the head. Angry thoughts bring about red and orange.

Valerie Hunt[4] investigated the reaction time of the HEF (see above figure). The subject was instructed to press a button as soon as she saw a light go on. Dr. Hunt used electrodes to measure the reaction time of the HEF, EEG electrodes to record from the brain, and an electrical-signal finger device to measure the reaction time of skeletal muscle, in this case the finger. The experimental data showed the HEF reacted in one-ten-thousandth of a second, the brain reacted in one-tenth of a second, while both the mind and the finger reacted in one-half of a second. So who is the decision maker? This startling data indicates the HEF is the decision-maker, the brain the decoder and motor output generator, and the finger the instrument of action or movement.

Neurophysiologists Benjamin Libet and Bertram Feinstein at Mount Zion Hospital in San Francisco measured the time it took for a touch stimulus on a patient's skin to reach the brain as an electrical signal[5]. The patient was also asked to push a button when he or she became aware of being touched. They found that the HEF registered the stimulus in one-ten-thousandth of a second after it occurred, and the patient pressed the button one-tenth of a second after the stimulus was applied. However, the patient didn't report being consciously aware of either the stimulus or pressing the button for almost one-half of a second. This meant that the decision to respond was being made by the patient's unconscious mind or the HEF. The patient's conscious awareness of the action is the slowest to respond. Even more disturbing, none of the patients Libet and Feinstein tested was aware that his unconscious mind had already caused him to push the buttons before he consciously decided to do so. Somehow his mind is creating an illusion that he consciously controlled the action even though he had not. This has caused some researchers to wonder if free will is an illusion.

Later studies have shown that one and one-half seconds before we *think* we "decide" to move one of our muscles, such as lift a finger, our brain has already started to generate the signals to accomplish the movement. *Who* is making the decision? Is it the conscious mind or something else? Hunt believes we have overrated the brain as the active ingredient in the relationship of a human to the world. It's just a real good computer. The aspects of the mind that have to do with creativity, imagination, spirituality, and decision-making are somewhere else. Her data suggests that the mind is not in the brain. It's in the HEF. Indeed, if the mind is in the HEF, it suggests that our awareness — the thinking, feeling part of ourselves — may not even be confined to the physical body, and there is considerable evidence to support this idea as well. The above studies suggest that the body may be just an illusory projection in a holographic universe. Physicist David Bohm[6] believes that even time itself is not absolute, but merely unfolds out of the implicate order. Research suggests that the linear division of time into past, present, and future may be just another construct of the mind.

These experiments clearly indicate that decisions are being made by the HEF and not the brain. It appears the spirit is the decision maker, the brain is the decoder and order giver, and the finger, in this case, is the executor of the action.

These data further confirmed my own hypotheses that telepathy originates from spirit and not the brain. It may explain why people can communicate with disembodied spirits of humans or animals. In addition, the speed of an answer to a question during telepathy is instantaneous; it receives the answer even before the question is finished coming out of a person's mouth, which correlates with the speed (one-ten-thousandth of a second) of the HEF response in the experiments described above.

Telepathic communication involves mental connection with spirit, and therefore, implies an elevation of awareness to unity consciousness. Thus, telepathy appears to be accomplished by transcending dualities and tapping into the universal mind.

The heart connection. The key element in entering the telepathic field and communicating with spirit is what animals call the heart connection. It is a band of energy that connects one being with another and is something a person can "see" with clarified inner vision. The energy band itself, has been investigated and described by scientists. Physicist David Bohm discovered non-random energy bands, invisible to the human eye, which form a cohesive pattern connecting all other bands in an otherwise chaotic field. Bohm believes these energy grids form a background from which all material forms obtain their patterns. He calls the grids the "implicate order," meaning that all potential future forms to be manifested in the physical realm already have their implied pattern in the universal field. As particles of matter combine with the implicate order, a physical form manifests, which he calls the "explicate order[7]."

In addition to their property as the structural basis of potential future forms as described by Bohm, the bands have certain elastic properties which allow for movement about without losing original contact with its home base. Sheldrake discovered that pigeons in a flock or group are in constant contact with all other members of the group allowing them to coordinate their flying so they stay together as a group even if some of the pigeons are several hundred meters away[8].

In a landmark study by Wayne Potts in 1980, the banking movements of large flocks of dunlins were examined[9]. Potts took films with very rapid exposures, so they could be slowed down to examine the way in which movements of flocks occurred. Analysis revealed that the movement was not exactly simultaneous, but started either from a single individual bird or from a few birds together. This signal, or initiation of movement within the flock, could start anywhere in the flock and the maneuvers passed through the flock like a wave radiating from the site of initiation. These waves took an average of only fifteen milliseconds (thousandths of a second) to pass from neighbor to neighbor. Sheldrake believes these coordinated movements occur within a morphogenetic field, where all members of the colony are bound together via these invisible bands. These findings reinforce the idea that animals in flocks act as a group mind with an oversoul as leader and coordinator.

When connecting with an animal telepathically, it is only necessary to connect with the person and then follow its heart connection to the animal. The animal does not have to be in the same room, the same city, or even in the same dimension (the afterlife). The energy bands remain intact even across dimensions and makes possible communication with spirit.

Psychics appear, in part, to connect with the deceased loved one in the same manner. Gary E. Schwartz, Ph.D and researchers from the University of Arizona conducted a study with four nationally recognized psychics — two men and two women[10]. The four conducted their usual psychic session with the same subject, a woman called Anne. To eliminate the possibility of reading the subject's body language, and to prevent any electrical or magnetic energy from being transferred to the psychics, a lead shield was placed between the psychic and subject. To guard against the psychic merely giving simple feedback from what the subject said, the subject was instructed to answer only with a "yes" or "no" and to give her name, "Anne." The subject and psychics were then connected to EEG, EKG electrodes, a body wrap that records breathing, and surface electrodes to the finger for recording parasympathetic activity. The results were the same in all psychics: the psychic had a physiological recording baseline "A" and the subject a baseline "B" which was different. As soon as the psychic said, "Hello, my name is John," and the subject said, "Hello, my name is Anne," the physiological responses of the psychic, i.e., baseline A, changed to match those of the subject, baseline B. Thus, all that was required to tune in to the subject was to connect with her voice. When the reading began and a spirit entity "came through," the psychic would ask the subject a question like, "Did your husband recently pass away, because I am getting a man with dark hair that identifies himself as your husband?" The subject answered "Yes." The EKG pattern then shifted to another pattern C, which was neither A or B. This was true for all four psychics. The investigators offered no explanation for this phenomenon[11].

My question is, how do you get a heart pattern from a sentient being? The only explanation I can offer is that the deceased spirit retains its HEF with all its energy patterns, attitudes, loves, hopes, desires and attachments when it enters the afterlife and these can be detected by the psychic as the entity engages in interdimensional communications with them.

When strong feelings of affection and attachment exist between an animal and its person, the energy bonds remain intact even across dimensions.

For the animal communicator, it becomes easy to pick up on an animal's personality, memories, thoughts and feelings and relate them to their person in this dimension. For me, personally, animals in spirit form appear as apparitions, i.e., I can see through them. If the animal is alive, it appears across the screen of my consciousness as a solid body. If the animal has been in the spirit world, I see only a static imprint of its former body, and then the animal quickly shows me what form it has reincarnated into in its current life. If I ask an animal to show me what it was in its previous life, it will quickly show me what the animal's body looked like. The client will then validate that, indeed, they had a dog or cat that looked like that some time ago.

Evidence for trace patterns across dimensions comes from an experiment performed in the early 1990's by Vladimir Poponin, from Moscow's Russian Academy of Sciences. A leading expert in the field of quantum biology, Poponin discovered a startling relationship between human tissue DNA and the quality of light, measured as photons[12]. He found that human DNA directly affects the physical world through a new and previously unknown field connecting the two.

Within a Bell jar or chBuddy (a glass jar shaped like a bell and with a lid that contains a spout for air to be vacuumed out) photons of light were measured in a controlled environment. After all the air was vacuumed out of the glass jar, it was sealed, and the patterns and spacing of light particles (photons) were measured, and it was shown to follow a random distribution as expected. Then a tissue sample with human DNA was placed inside the chBuddy (the glass jar). The patterns of photons within the jar began to fall into a new pattern resembling the crests and troughs of a wave (a sine wave). The DNA was influencing the photons, shaping them into the regularity of a smooth wave through an unknown invisible force.

When the tissue containing the DNA was removed from the chBuddy, and the air inside the chBuddy vacuumed out once more, the photons within the chBuddy did not go back to random activity; rather, they intuitively retained the wave form of the DNA tissue. Poponin writes that he and his associate researchers were "forced to accept the working hypothesis that some new field structure is being excited." The presence of the tissue, once inside the chBuddy, created a field structure by some invisible and unknown force. That pattern remained in the absence of the tissue, despite the fact that the chBuddy had been flushed and the air vacuumed out once more. He later termed the phenomenon the "DNA phantom effect[13]."

Dr. Poponin states, "We believe this discovery has tremendous significance for the explanation and deeper understandings of the mechanisms underlying subtle energy phenomena including many of the observed alternative healing phenomena." Poponin continues to say that "It seems very plausible that the DNA phantom effect is an example of subtle energy manifestation in which direct human influence is not involved." Poponin's data provide both the qualitative and quantitative data that are crucial for the development of a "New unified nonlinear quantum field theory which must include the physical theory of consciousness."

Is it possible that the psychic or telepath is detecting the residual "field structures" that once belonged to a living being, whether human, animal, plant or any other form? If so, then perhaps connection and communication with all forms of life which existed in the past is still possible. Application of the right technique to access these subtle energies may serve to open a door to the past; a kind of time travel, so to speak.

Telepathy, morphogenetic fields and the interconnectedness of life.

What makes all this possible? Researchers believe that the universe is made up of a background fabric which enables us to perceive the physical world as separate, although all things are intricately connected on many levels. The background fabric, termed the "morphic field" by Sheldrake and "implicate order" by Bohm form the basis of the energy structure that provides for the potentiality of any material manifestation of physical objects occurring in the "explicate" or unfolded order.

Further, quantum physics has shed new light on the simultaneity of time, meaning that quantum waves of energy that make up our physical universe can exist in more than one dimension at the same time. Bohm's assertion that human consciousness has its source in the implicate order implies that all humans possess the ability to access the future. Research indicates from sixty to sixty-eight percent of all precognitions (premonitions) occur during dreaming. Because our dreaming self is deeper in the psyche than our conscious awake self - and closer to the "primal ocean" in which past, present and future become one — it may be easier to access information about future events. Sheldrake believes these fields are the basis of interconnections not only of space but also in time. A wide range of unexplained intuitive powers of humans and animals may be explainable in terms of the characteristics of morphic fields:

1. Morphic fields link members of social groups and continue to connect them even when they are far apart. These invisible bonds act as channels for telepathic communication between animals and animals, people and animals, and people and people.

2. These links, acting like invisible elastic bands, also underlie the sense of direction that enables animals and people to find each other.

3. Animals imprint on their home environment

or on other significant places are linked to these places by morphic fields. Through these connections they can be pulled or attracted back toward familiar places, enabling them to navigate across unfamiliar terrain. The sense of direction given by these morphic fields underlies both homing and migration.

4. Morphic fields link animals to the objects of their intentions and could help to explain psychokinetic phenomena.
5. Morphic fields link animals to the objects of their attention and through these perceptual fields animals can influence what they are looking at. These fields underlie the sense of being stared at[14].

Sheldrake has outlined common features of animal telepathy:

1. Animal telepathy involves the influence of animals on other animals independently of the known senses.
2. Telepathy usually occurs between closely related animals that are part of the same social group — in other words, it takes place between animals that are bonded with each other.
3. In schools, flocks, herds, packs, and other social groups, telepathic communication may plan an important role in the coordination of the activity of the group as a whole.
4. At least in birds and mammals, telepathy has to do with emotions, needs, and intentions. Feelings communicated telepathically include fear, alarm, excitement, calls for help, calls to go to a particular place, anticipation of arrivals, departures, and distress and dying[14].

These features pertain to human telepathy as well, especially in dramatic cases of human precognitions concerning accidents or deaths. He points out that morphic fields can explain the interconnectedness of not only groups, but between individual beings, the trees, plants, and even the earth itself. This interconnectedness can be disrupted by cataclysmic events such as earthquakes. The impending quake disrupts the morphic field in such a way that animals have been reported to exhibit strange and bizarre behaviors. For example, in the 1970's the Chinese State Seismological Bureau issued a warning that a serious earthquake could be expected in the province of Liaoning within the next few years. That same year, a few months later, snakes came out of hibernation, crawled from their burrows, and froze to death on the snow-covered surface. Rats appeared in the open in large groups and were so confused they were able to be caught by hand. Hours before the earthquake actually occurred, geese flew wildly, crashed into trees while dogs barked as if mad. Pigs began to bite each other or dig beneath fences, chickens refused to go into their coops, and cattle ran away. Rats and small rodents came out in the open and acted intoxicated. This mass disorientation of animals at times of seismic fluctuation has been used as a predictor of impending quakes by other countries, including the United States[15].

The earth and its human and non-human animals appear to be interwoven in a morphic energy field, which, under certain conditions, can be accessed both in dreams and other precognitive conditions. Sensitivity to tuning in to the subtle energies of this field appears to be possible for intuitives, telepaths, psychics, and experienced meditators who seem to agree that the prerequisite for such reception is a quiet mind and a willingness to let go of conventional notions of human/animal communications.

CHAPTER TWELVE

Plants, Trees, Rocks, and Mother Earth

"Take a moment to consider this: Look at your
hand. Now look at the light streaming from the lamp
beside you. And at the dog resting at your feet. You
are not merely made of the same thing, **you are the
same thing.** One thing. Unbroken. One enormous
something that has extended its uncountable arms
and appendages into all the apparent objects, atoms,
restless oceans, and twinkling stars in the cosmos."
Michael Talbot, *Holographic Universe*[1]

Love all creation. The whole and every grain of
sand in it. Love every leaf, and every ray of light. Love
the plants. Love the animals. Love everything. If you
love everything you will perceive the Divine Mystery in
all things. Once you perceive it you will comprehend it
better every day. And you will come, at last, to love the
whole world with an all embracing love.
Matthew Fox, *One River, Many Wells*[2]

Mother Earth, a Living Being.

When you learn how to connect with the telepathic field,
everything opens up for you. It's not merely connecting with just
animals. You can connect and have an in depth, heart-to-heart
conversation with anything that is alive, and everything is alive.
Mother Earth herself is a living entity, a living spirit, a living
being, with an energy field surrounding it, the same as any other
object.

Let me illustrate. A conversation with a rock told me much
about life and civilization. As I walked along a beautiful wooded
section of Cleveland MetroParks, an interesting looking stone
caught my eye and I picked it up. It was stratified; that is, it had
many layers. I sat down and became quiet in order to talk to the
rock. I began with the usual question: What do you like about

being a rock? Knowing it was a fellow being I asked a deeper question, Will you tell me about your life and relationship to the earth and all other life? I was astounded by and have never forgotten its answer. The rock said that the earth remodels itself according to the attitude of humankind. Humankind exists within the earth's energy field. If humankind's attitudes are negative or hostile, the earth will remodel itself to provide a hostile environment so humans feel at home. Remodeling takes the form of volcanic eruptions, earthquakes, storms, floods, and other natural disasters that affect masses of people and Earth's other inhabitants. If humankind's attitude is benevolent, that's another story. The earth will create a nurturing, beautiful, fruitful environment so that humankind can survive and feel at home. So our thoughts, which are more than just thoughts, but also things, create the world in which we live — hostile or gentle.

Native Americans are very much in tune with Mother Nature and Mother Earth. They feel the vibrations beneath their feet; they feel the pain of trees, plants, and animals that are starving for clean air to breathe and clean water to drink. They hold ceremonies to invoke nature's spirits who can help to restore the delicate balance of nature and ensure the survival of all life on Earth.

Consider the following consultation: I was doing a film shoot for a workshop video on animal communication at a place called Buttermilk Falls situated within the Cleveland MetroParks. The MetroParks is a land preserve set aside by early settlers for the conservation of nature. It is a circular strip of land surrounding the Cleveland area and is sometimes beautifully referred to as The Emerald Necklace, as it appears from an aerial view. A series of parks begin at Lake Erie, loop around and within several counties, and close at Lake Erie, much like a necklace laid out circular on a flat surface. Buttermilk Falls is a small, pretty, and slowly flowing falls located in an area of the necklace called North Chagrin Reservation, east of Cleveland. The slate at the base of the falls had been cut away in layers and removed for commercial building projects. The waterfall created a peaceful and pleasing sound while I gazed upon it and tried to communicate with it. It was very happy to communicate with me. I asked it how it liked being a waterfall. It answered that it enjoyed being what it is. The reflection of light upon it made it a beautiful and constant show of nature within its particular environment. My question of whether the slate rock could perceive the differences in the seasons was answered in a strange way. The rock explained that in winter, it pulls back its energy and goes into a sort of hibernation and rest. It is rejuvenated by an energy received upward from the earth. In spring, this energy is brought forth and surrounds the entire area. Positive and healing energy comes to that place. I was unaware this kind of activity occurred in nature. I thanked the waterfall and the slate for their communication, which left a deep impression on me. Perhaps Mother Earth replenishes all life in much the same way.

I had an occasion to speak to another rock that was positioned behind my house. As I focused on it, I found it to be a very interesting being. It told me that its strata represented many periods, many experiences in its life. It said that it had been witness to at least seven ice ages and that it was part of what was once a greater rock formation. It explained that when the glaciers began to melt and move surface materials, it broke off from the greater portion and floated downstream with many other fragments of the same greater rock and came to rest on the ground behind where my house now stands. I asked the rock if it was happy. It answered that it is perfectly content to be wherever Mother Nature puts it. Each life form is an experience in itself, and it tries to absorb as much as it can from each experience — experience here meaning location.

Like animals, the rock appeared to live in the present. It simply would experience life as it is. It needn't worry about the future or think of the past. It was but a part of a great universal plan and was grateful to be so. I ended the communication by thanking the rock for the new knowledge it gave me.

I couldn't help wondering why we humans can't be as content as a rock to be a part of nature and this ever-evolving plan. Why do humans have to make life so complicated? Why can't we just be?

One of the first animal-communication workshops I conducted was held in my sister Flo's back yard. Flo had chosen to continue living in the house our parents built. She was an avid gardener whose yard looked like a showplace where she so loved working and relaxing. Flo seemed to be able to make anything grow and thrive. I, unfortunately, can't. I'd been very impressed with her garden and the lush growth, which became more vivid to me during the workshop. One of the exercises involved each of us finding a plant to communicate with. I picked a small, delicate-looking plant — which I later discovered was thyme — growing in the herb garden adjacent to the back of the house. I opened a communication with it. It said it was very pleased to be in what it experienced as a very happy garden in which all its life forms got along with each other. It said that part of the energy of the garden was Flo's and part was my father's. She inherited her love of gardening from our dad. I asked the plant the usual round of questions. It identified itself as a male entity. I asked it to show me its perception of God. It's probably the best explanation I've ever heard and it goes like this: everything is light, sound and vibration. It showed me, through the screen of my consciousness, bars of music, and it said every sound has its own vibration, attracting particles of matter from the earth to create a life form. It showed me a musical note being formed. Each form is perfectly orchestrated with every other form to create a sound. He called it the Sound of the Universe.

You humans refer to it as the Celestial Sound.

He then showed me what reminded me of the big bang, though he did not use that term. He said that from the beginning of time, referring to the human construct of time, every segment of our history had a different sound or melody and each sound represented some stage of development or evolution of the cosmos. Each melody was part of a song being sung by God and there are many songs. I asked, "Did God create the sound?"

God is both Creator and creation. It is both the Maker of the sound and the Sound Itself.

I was surprised at his sophisticated answer and told him so.

You humans go wrong when you assign human characteristics to God. God is not a human being. You think that God must be like you. But God is not like you. You are like God.

I asked for further clarification.

Your essence, your divinity, your spirit is God. There is only one Soul, and everything in existence is the expression of it.

Later that day as we were practicing communicating, I had a conversation with the next-door neighbors' plum tree located on the property line between Flo's yard and her neighbors'. I remembered that the neighbors' yard was open land before they built on it around 1952. My father used it as a vegetable garden, in addition to the one planted behind our house. The neighbor man, who was handy around the house and in gardening like my dad, had planted the plum tree. At the time of this workshop, the plum tree had been in the ground for many years and was showing signs of aging and dying. In fact, the new owners pruned it back drastically, cutting off much dead material. The tree told me it had been the family tree of those who had first built on the property and raised their family there, the mother and widow remaining in the house until about 1996. The tree said that when the mother — then in a nursing home — dies, it will also die. Our family knew the neighbors well, almost as additional family members and as time passed, Flo and the widow remained close friends. Holding true to the promise of following the mother in death, the plum tree was dead the following spring. The mother had passed away the previous October.

Healing From the Earth.

In addition to this interesting memory, there is another associated with this area of land. When I was a child and Flo was just a baby, my grandmother, who owned and lived on a small patch of farmland about an hour's drive away, would visit us. Sometime during her visit, she would lay down directly on the soil in this area of our yard, near that plum tree. There was a small pathway there joining the two properties. I asked my mother why Grandma did this, and she replied, "Because it helps relieve her arthritis." As a small child, I didn't really understand; but, later as a scientist, I learned that people used to do this type of thing in order to absorb directly from the earth its minerals, particularly magnesium, to help in the metabolism of calcium and healthy bone. My grandmother was a Hungarian immigrant and spoke very little English. Somehow, in her wisdom, she knew that what she needed for her improved health was in and from the earth. This memory became for me a validation of what Buttermilk Falls had told me about absorbing energy from the earth.

I decided to communicate with the soil and was surprised to discover that my father's energy had become part of the soil, though his body was not buried there. He so loved his home and gardens that his essence became part of its energy, particularly in the roses he planted around the perimeter of the house so many years ago. It's phenomenal, at least to me, a non-gardener, that those climbing roses, well over sixty years old, are still thriving and blooming faithfully and abundantly every spring, in spite of Cleveland's very harsh winters.

When I talked with the soil, I asked about my grandmother and why she did as she did with it.

The earth provides everything life needs. There is nothing it cannot provide for life to exist.

Warren Grossman, a psychologist from the Cleveland area and author of *To Be Healed by the Earth*[3], offers evidence of this apparent truth. Grossman contracted a severe case of hepatitis while visiting Brazil. He thought it was incurable and was going to die. One day, needing to relieve his body of the extreme discomfort of inflammation, he lay down upon the ground hoping to cool his body. While in this position, he saw waves of energy coming up from the earth. Grossman claims to have been freed of the hepatitis and its effects on his body by this energy. He remains free and clear of hepatitis to this day. He now holds seminars and workshops wherein people can be taught how to absorb and use the energy of the earth to heal their bodies.

Grossman claims that the healing effect can be achieved by sitting on the ground near the base of a tree, positioning the spine to make contact with the tree trunk. He says he can perceive the energy of the earth rising up and into the tree and then feeling the penetration into the spine.

There's something about relinquishing a fear of death that raises consciousness to new heights. When Grossman thought he was going to die, he lost his fear of death and simply desired to relieve his discomfort. Similarly, to those who have had near death experiences, including myself, something happens when they let themselves be completely open to the universe and what will come. Losing the fear of death appears to be a key element in raising the level of consciousness.

Consider a communication I had with a tree in Point Reyes while attending Penelope's workshop: part of the forest around Penelope's house was destroyed by a fire. I wondered what it would be like to talk to one of the burned out trees. It turned out to be a very moving experience. My question to the tree was: "What do you have to teach me today?"

Look at me. Really look. The part that is above ground has much burned tissue. My roots (spirit) *are untouched. I have the ability to completely regenerate and replace every cell of my life. Look at my new branches.*

I could see new branches forming from the stump of the tree.

I am tighter, closer, and denser than before; more refined, more efficient at processing nutrition and energy than before. I can provide more shade and oxygen to the earth's inhabitants. Can you see that I am the mirror of your struggles with the physical dimension? Come now and embrace me, my daughter, refresh yourself whenever you wish. I long for you to breathe in my life-giving oxygen. Give me your carbon dioxide so I can perform my function. Look at me and see life renewing itself.

"What can I give to you?"

Give me your appreciation. Take the garden hose and sprinkle water on me so I can refresh myself.

I turned on the garden hose and sprayed the tree for a few minutes.

"What can I give to others?"

Be not afraid to speak your truth. It is time for the Divine Mother to reveal her power. People are searching for the feminine aspect of the divine, but do not know how to find her. Your words will be carried much farther than you think. They will lead the earth children back to their true home. Our earth mother is calling all things back to herself. The earth of the past will not continue in its present form. Enlightenment will replace illusion. There will be no deceit. All minds will be open. No untruth will remain hidden.

"I'm not sure what you mean. Can you explain?"

No crimes will occur because no deceit will exist. Everything will be open for all to know.

"Are you talking about everyone having access to the universal mind?"

Yes, it will be like the speed of telepathy. These same channels will transport truth instantaneously. Beings will be able to transport themselves from one place to another by love alone. Fossil fuels will no longer be needed. The concepts of time and space will no longer exist. It will be realized and understood all are connected to everything in the universe. All will be one.

Water also has an interesting story to tell. I recall a story while I was in telepathic training in Rochester, New York. My roommate, Abby, had a very moving communication with a stream running through the farm. The stream said to her that all it could see from its perspective were faces, faces, faces. The stream originated from an underground spring and emptied into a larger waterway. The stream said, *Humans sometimes see their faces reflected in the water. Do they not understand that they are water?*

It's true. Over 90% of the human body is composed of water.

Do they not understand that they and I are one?

I guess I never looked at it that way. Yes, humans and water are one. Earth is the water planet.

Dr. Masaru Emoto has studied and photographed molecules of water[4]. He discovered that crystals formed in frozen water reveal changes when specific, concentrated thoughts are directed toward them. He found that water from clear springs and water that has been exposed to loving words shows brilliant, complex, and snowflake patterns. In contrast, polluted water, or water exposed to negative thoughts forms incomplete, asymmetrical patterns with dull colors. He suggests that human attitude is an important factor in healing.

Emoto's studies of water support the conversation I had with the rocks, about the earth remodeling itself according to the attitude of mankind.

The earth provides clean spring water to ensure the survival of all life. Water is a life-giving entity, as precious as blood, sustaining life on the earth. Water is the life-giving source of all our food, including vegetables, fruit, and yes, even animal flesh. It is the mother that nurtures all fish in the oceans and streams.

Water is a great gift of the earth and should be revered and thanked for its contribution to the sustenance of life. I thought about how little respect we've given our waterways. When we hurt nature, we're really hurting ourselves. We are taking away the very essence of what keeps us alive.

CHAPTER THIRTEEN

Animals and Medical Research

The use of animals in medical research is probably the most misunderstood issue by the general public. Anti-vivisection groups and organizations claiming to be against medical research because it is inhumane to animals should talk with people who do this type of research. I've done medical research with animals for 25 years. I can tell you that in 25 years, there have been only three instances in which I've seen animals not treated properly.

There are very strict laws governing the use of animals for research. Each university or research facility has an Institutional Animal Care and Use Committee (IACUC) which enforces these laws. The committee consists of physicians, scientists, veterinarians, hospital administrators, animal facility caretakers, and lay people.

Before a single animal may be used for research, the researcher must write what is called an Animal Protocol specifically for the particular research project being conducted. It must consist of what the research is about, its purpose, the medical question being addressed in the research, how many animals will be used, how many studies will be performed, whether the research is a repeat of another study, the intended discovery, and the expected outcome. It describes housing needs of the animals, how many are to be housed in the same cage, what will be done for the animal if it experiences any more than momentary pain or distress (i.e., the stick of a needle for injection).

It is very difficult, because of today's laws, to have any research experiments approved if they will cause any pain whatsoever to the animals. The Animal Protocol must explain what will be done with the carcasses of the animals at the completion of the experiments. Generally, the carcasses must be returned to the Resource Facility for disposal. On occasion, if an unexpected death occurs, the veterinarian will be asked to perform an autopsy and may send tissue to an outside laboratory for evaluation.

Investigations follow in unusual cases, i.e., an appreciable number of animals died during testing, or an animal, such as a dog, developed an infection, or other unusual conditions. Until any questionable conditions are explained satisfactorily, the research is suspended.

For example, if thirty animals were used, but after the first ten none showed the expected results and the researcher didn't terminate testing at that point himself, an investigation takes place. The Protocol is resubmitted to the committee, which carefully considers the issues and makes recommendations. Experts on the committee will discuss and evaluate the clinical significance or scientific merit of the particulars of the Protocol that involve their own field of expertise. If there is no committee member who is expert in a particular field involved in the research, one will always be located and asked to serve as an outside reviewer for that study. No issues are left unattended or ignored.

Before even one animal can be purchased from the facility, the Protocol must be submitted for approval to the agency funding the research project (e.g., The National Institutes of Health or The American Heart Association). The committee or the funding agency will further scrutinize the Protocol. The committee will search research literature to see if the studies have been performed previously and investigate the scientific merit of the research project. Unless the Animal Protocol goes through all the channels and is properly approved, the researcher may not obtain any animals from the Animal Resource Facility.

For pilot studies, when researchers have several ideas and want to test their hypotheses on a single animal, the same protocol procedure must be conducted. The same stringent laws apply. The research must be discussed and evaluated as to whether the hypotheses are worth a full study.

An animal facility is set up according to several criteria. Animals of the same species, for example, rats, are placed in rooms separate from mice, dogs, rabbits, or cats. Some animals require a virus-antibody-free environment and are isolated from others. Other animals, mice, for example, who are exposed to pathogens may be housed individually in micro-isolators with special ventilation systems to prevent the pathogen from becoming airborne and entering the common ventilation system. There is seven-day coverage for the facility with appropriate staff — veterinarians, supervisors, animal technicians, and investigative staff.

How the Animals Feel About Research.

In 1990, when I first began communicating telepathically with animals (when my cat Frosty was ill), I became concerned about using animals in my medical research. I discussed my concerns with both Anna and Becky. I was of the mind that if animals didn't want to be used as research subjects, I would leave animal research and find another profession. I didn't want to ignore, even for the sake of medical research, the wishes of the animals. Both Anna and Becky communicated with my laboratory rats and I was very surprised at their responses. The rats said they knew before their incarnation that they would be used in medical research and that also they had been with me in prior lifetimes and I was very kind to them. They were honored to be a part of my current research. Their only request of me was that I would not cause them physical pain and that I would inform them of what I was going to do to them before I did it. They felt they were making a contribution to human health and wellness of humans around the world. Of course, I complied with their wishes. Before any experimentation, I would go to the Animal Resource Facility and communicate with the rats, telling them what I planned to do and what would be involved.

Once I went to the animal room with a troubled heart, because I felt that one of the protocols outlined in the grant was too stressful for the animals. One of the rats in a cage came forward and asked what was bothering me. I told the rat that I thought this particular protocol was a little too harsh and I wished there could be another way. He asked me, *What are you trying to find out?* I answered that I was trying to discover how animals acquire sleep apnea, which is a pause in breathing during sleep causing serious complications including hypoxemia, vascular disease, and cognitive dysfunction in humans. I explained the hypothesis.

I don't know why you want to do it that way; that's not how it works.

"Okay. How does it work?"

We get sick when our sleep is interrupted when we're babies.

I pondered the rat's explanation. I knew from developmental psychology that anything done to humans early in life will remain with them, in some form, for their entire lives. So, from a neurological and psychological development aspect, the rat's response could be true. I wondered what could happen in a home that could cause sleep disruption inducing such a disorder. It would have to be something occurring naturally in the home. The only hypothesis I came up with was the possibility that the baby's sleep was disturbed by noise or tactile contact during the first few weeks of its life. It also had something to do with thermoregulation, that is, the ability to maintain its own body temperature. Thermoregulation does not occur naturally in a baby until it is about one month of age. In rats, it occurs after approximately the first two weeks of life. A mother rat will make a nest around her babies to keep them warm during the time she is away from them for eating or grooming. If the researcher removes or destroys the nest within the first two weeks of life, the mother will immediately reconstruct the nest. If this is repeated after the first two weeks, the mother will not reconstruct the nest.

I was able to use an instrument called an infrared thermister to measure the body heat of animals. The normal temperature of a baby rat is 38.5° to 39°C. If the babies were huddled around the mother, their temperatures measured 41°C. Away from the mother, their temperatures fell to 34°C, which is a very dangerous level. The ensuing hypothermia initiates a compensatory reduction in breathing and metabolism in an effort to maintain life under dire circumstances. It is at the 34° C temperature that other rodents, like hamsters, suddenly fall into a state of hibernation.

I designed the experiment so that I could interrupt sleep in newborn baby rats during the first week of life. I did this by making a sound and by petting their bodies for seven days and then let them grow up under normal conditions. They grew to adulthood and did develop sleep apnea. The first two weeks of a rat's life have certain "sensitive periods" in which the respiratory control system is formed. Sleep is an important component in the assimilation and retention of new information into the brain. Disrupting their sleep even for only a few minutes was enough to prevent new breathing patterns to be recorded into brain memory[1]. I also found that when apneic rats produced offspring, the offspring also had the disorder with no experimental intervention. This suggested to me that the breathing disorder was transferred from mother to pup in utero.

Mutual respect and cooperation between animal and experimenter produced an answer to the medical question at hand. Since then, I always communicated to my research animals what was going on in the laboratory. They were fully cooperative. And as I had promised, they never felt the pain of even a needle stick. I gave them a small amount of halothane (an inhalant gas) as a pre-anesthetic prior to the injection in order to anesthetize them prior to euthanize them without pain.

I would like to comment on medical research using animals. People are often offended by what they don't understand. Research protest groups say that medical research on animals is terrible and shouldn't be done. This just isn't correct. Medical research is done very carefully and with great scrutiny by people who have the greatest minds in the country. I personally worked with rats, hamsters and guinea pigs. People who work with animals in the laboratory love the animals and treat them as pets. I don't know of any researcher who worked with rats and didn't love them.

I'd like to tell a delightful true story. In a previous life one of my cats, Nanda, was a research hamster, Bobby, in my lab. The experiment Bobby was a part of was unsuccessful and he could not be used in another experiment. Bobby was so adorable I just couldn't bring myself to euthanize him. I decided to keep him in a cage in my lab and every morning I would share my donut with him. He got to be a darling friend of mine. I would put him into a clear plastic exercising ball so he could move around the lab and have some fun. Staff would see him and greet him as a pet. On holiday weekends when no one was around the lab to feed him, I would take him home. There he would play with my cat, Puff, who'd been domesticated (as much as a cat can be) from day one, and didn't see the hamster as prey. The two would snuggle and fall asleep. Bobby lived quite long for a hamster — about three years — and died of old age. We held a funeral and buried him in the forest behind our house. A year later, Puff died, and four months after that, Puff returned to me as another orange kitty.

During the time I was searching to find my reincarnated Frosty, I saw a cat at an animal shelter that looked exactly like Puff had looked, except that much of his long golden fur had been shaved due to entangled burrs and he had a bad eye infection. The vet at the shelter treated him. I don't know how, but I saw in this cat an energy that I recognized and could not resist adopting him. I brought him home and called Becky, the communicator, explaining my feelings. She told me that this cat had known me, too, as one of my former pets. She said he was not a cat at the time and I told her I never had a pet that wasn't a cat. She said he had a people name. Then I remembered. "Bobby?" I asked, and as soon as I said the name, the cat's face lit up. Yes! This cat had been Bobby, my lab hamster!

He told Becky that he wanted to come back into a cat's body and wanted it to look just like Puff's and that's just what happened. He further told her that he was not appointed to me in this life, but his persons never loved him and when he was about twelve weeks old threw him out of the window of a moving car to dispose of him. He fell down into a ravine and was badly hurt. I asked him how he survived the winter. He said a woman took pity on him and would leave food and water outside for him. When his eyes became infected, she called the Lake County Humane Society and they picked him up. He said that his return to me as a cat was orchestrated by my late husband and the angels. Before I named him, I asked him what name he would like. He didn't want a people name this time; he wanted to be named after royalty. I made a list of names and read them to him and he rejected each name until I said the name "Nanda," a Hindu word meaning "sweet boy child." He said, *That's it, I am Nanda!* Nanda turned out to be a great communicator, and helps out with my workshops. Sometimes he even butts in on my consultations, saying, *You didn't understand the dog Mommy, he meant such and such.* When I introduced him to the family of cats, Puff said, *He looks just like me in my old body.* So, yes, one of my research animals actually *chose* to reincarnate and came back to me as a pet.

CHAPTER FOURTEEN

The Healing Power of Animals

"Ignorance is the supreme disease. When one banishes ignorance he also banishes the causes of all physical, mental, and spiritual disease. Wisdom is the greatest cleanser."

Swami Sri Yukteswar
In: Man's Eternal Quest[1]

Animals as Healers.

In the times of ancient Egyptians, stories of priestesses and their "familiars," (i.e., animals) proficient at healing illnesses in humans were both legendary and common. According to folklore, the priestess would listen to the patient's physical complaints, and instruct the animal (usually a cat), which supposedly possessed empathic abilities, to take upon itself the illness freeing it from the patient. The animal's spirit took the basis of the illness from the patient's spirit, making it whole once more. The animal's spirit, which was believed to be capable of transdimensional travel, elevated its consciousness to a high spiritual level, and was able to "cast off" the patients' illness by raising the vibratory energy of the illness to a higher spiritual plane where physical imperfection does not exist. The priestesses believed that thoughts, attitudes, and ignorance of spirit were responsible for the afflictions of the human body.

I asked animals to tell me how they go about healing themselves from illness or injury. They say that when they are ill, they utilize everything in their environment to bring about healing to themselves. They "intuitively" know what plants or herbs to seek out; they find a stream of fresh spring water and claim to detect mineral springs which contain certain minerals they need for healing of particular ailments. Their bodies produce chemicals that reduce their activity, and make them assume a restful stance so healing may occur. I can personally testify to their statements.

In 1982, I did my doctoral dissertation on "Stimulation Produced Analgesia and Suppression of Behavior in the Rat[2]." In the study, I placed stimulating needle electrodes in an area of the brain called the central gray, an area of gray matter surrounding the cerebral aqueduct in rats. Just ten seconds of electrical stimulation at a current at 0.5 millivolts produced long-lasting analgesia. The analgesia was completely reversible by the opiate antagonist, Naloxone. However, the sedation, which included a reduction in heart rate, breathing, locomotion and EEG activity, was not reversible and continued to suppress behavior for several hours or days. When handled, the animal was limp, docile, and its muscle strength so weak that it could not cling to a wire grid placed at a 45 degree angle for more than one second without sliding off. Rats ordinarily have the ability to climb and hang upside-down from branches and so on, because they have a long rectus abdominus muscle extending from the first thoracic vertebra to the pelvis. In humans, the rectus abdominus muscle ends at the end of the rib cage. The sedation appears to have shut down or put on minimal usage, major organ systems used for everyday activity, so the healing process could take precedence. Much has been published about the presence of endogenous opiates, termed endorphins by pharmacologists and other interested investigators.

Animals that heal humans. Many animals tell me that they provide healing energy to various areas of their person's body simply by laying down near the affected area. Their persons confirm that, indeed, their pet always seems to go right to the very spot that is hurting. It is no coincidence that many of the consultations I do with animals include healing of their person's physical body as a part of the pet's mission. Is it possible that animals intuitively know how to influence or directly affect the person's HEF in such a way as to promote healing? Animals don't think about it in those terms, they simply say, *I am here to heal my person.* When I inquire how that is accomplished, they say, *I just go to the spot where it hurts, and try to make it better.*

Persons who practice vibrational medicine and energy healing in their homes tell me that it is very common for their own pets to jump on top of their massage tables and sit next to the area of the body of the patient being healed. How they are drawn to the exact spot is a mystery. Animals say that they can "see" certain uneven energy waves emanating from the affected area and they are drawn to it. I can conceive of an experiment in which a patient lies on a table and their aura is videotaped. Then an animal is allowed to jump on the table and enter the patient's auric space. After the animal departs, the aura would be videotaped again, and the pre- and post-animal influence on the area videotapes compared.

Therapy animals. There is another way that animals heal humans. In recent years, it has become more and more popular to take specially trained therapy animals into hospitals, nursing homes, and other rehabilitation facilities to do animal therapy on patients. Patients report feeling better after interacting with dogs, cats, ferrets, and even birds in rehabilitation settings. I couldn't find any studies which objectively measured outcomes of animal therapy, but I have seen attitudes of patients towards their illnesses change remarkably. The only answer I can provide comes from my understanding of the relationship of children and their pets.

Children regard their pets as fellow beings in their interactions. The pet is probably the only relationship the child has, or ever will have, that is uncensored. The notion of unconditional love is at its best when referring to animals. Love and acceptance are primal factors in the child's world and provide a safe ground for fantasies about the future. Children can dream of, and play with anyone or anything in this accepting environment. The pet is a willing accomplice to the fun. Likewise, when a therapy dog comes in contact with a patient, it is my belief that this communication brings the patient back to a simpler time, when it was regarded as a whole person just as he/she was. This powerful and positive regard sets the stage for the patients, now afflicted, to step out of their mode of self-pity, and sort of re-invent themselves within the current context. The animal provides them with unconditional support and acceptance and opens the door to new ideas and plans. Therapy animals may be the spark of hope patients need to restore their mental and physical wellness.

Healing and the human energy field. We have seen in the previous chapters that physical illness and distress can be detected in the aura or HEF. Because an illness can appear in the HEF weeks and even months before it appears in the body, many psychics believe that disease actually originates in the HEF. This suggests that the field is in some way more primary than the physical body and functions as a kind of blueprint from which the body gets its structural cues. To put it another way, the HEF may be the body's own version of an implicate order.

Achterberg and Siegel (cited in Talbot)[3] found that some patients are already "imaging" their illnesses months before the illnesses manifest in their bodies. But as we have seen, ideas that are prominent in our thoughts can quickly manifest as images or patterns in the HEF. It follows that if the HEF is a blueprint that guides and molds the body, it may be that by imaging an illness even unconsciously and repeatedly reinforcing its presence in the field, we are, in effect, somehow programming the body to manifest the illness.

Similarly, this same dynamic linkage between mental images, the HEF, and the physical body may be one of the reasons imagery and visualization can also reverse and heal the body.

Richard Gerber, MD, who has investigated the medical implications of the body's subtle energy fields, believes that the etheric body is a holographic energy template that guides the growth and development of the physical body[4]. This idea is consistent with such faith-based religious healing beliefs including those of Mary Baker Eddy of Christian Science and Charles and Myrtle Fillmore of Unity Church of Christianity.

Energy healer Eric Perl, DC[5] claims that he is able to connect with this morphogenetic field to reconnect the patient with its primal being and bring about healing. He explains this ability by the principles outlined by Sheldrake. Perl claims that this energy can be activated by one healer in another by merely holding his hands over theirs.

Paramahansa Yogananda, an Indian Guru who came to the United States in the early 1920's, tells the story of an Indian Sadhu (holy man) who understood the interdimensional relationship between body and spirit:

An amazing case.

There is a case on record, in the files of French and other European doctors, of a man named Sadhu Haridas — in the court of emperor Ranjit Singh of India — who was able to separate his energy and consciousness from his body and then connect the two again after several months. His body was buried underground and watch was kept over the spot, day and night, for months. At the end of this time, his body was exhumed and examined by the European doctors who pronounced him dead. After a few minutes, however, he opened his eyes and regained control over all the functions of his body; and lived for many years more. He had learned, by practice, how to control all the involuntary functions of his body and mind. He was a spiritual scientist who experimented with prescribed methods for learning the truth of cosmic law. As a result he was in a position to demonstrate the truth of the theory of the changelessness of personal identity and the eternal nature of the life principle."

Man's Eternal Quest[6]

Energy healing and vibrational medicine have become part of what is loosely called holistic healing. Although I, personally, have not witnessed any actual healing in individuals by these methods, I cannot say that it doesn't work. My idea of proof of healing would be objective findings on x-ray films or seeing cancer cells in a tissue culture petrie dish mutate back into healthy cells by virtue of Reiki or prayer alone. Such a study is taking place at the Cleveland Clinic Foundation. Cancer cells in a petrie dish are being exposed to daily treatments of Reiki. The preliminary findings suggest that Reiki is having a restorative effect on the cells, but it is too soon to confirm the data.

Objective evidence for healing by thought alone comes from a demonstration of Chinese medicine. The subject is a patient with a large kidney stone. The stone is continuously monitored by ultrasound while a video camera taped three doctors sending intentions to the patient's kidney to break up and dissolve the stone. As remarkable as it may seem, one could see the stone breaking up and dissolving on the ultrasound screen, while the three doctors shook their hands at the patient attempting to force their intentions on the stone.

CHAPTER FIFTEEN

The Big Picture

"Do not judge by what you see on the surface, but develop an inner vision and insight into spiritual cause and effect. Then you will know that you can judge no man."

Paramahansa Yogananda
The Quiet Mind: Sayings of White Eagle[1]

My journey into the animal mind started out as a mystery and scientific investigation and quickly turned into a transcendent and mystical journey into inter-dimensional communication. As for many others who have taken this journey, my life is forever changed. It is like going on vacation to a beautiful place where everyone and everything in existence there operates from a base of pure love. The experience in this special place is one of total understanding and acceptance, and it is filled with beings waiting at your fingertips to offer assistance. It's a place that once you visit, you'll want to return again and again until you can make this place — that is, this level of consciousness — your home. The journey itself is nothing less than a venture inward to the core of life itself, and the rediscovery of the divine in all creation and in one's self.

Anyone who has ever had a relationship with a pet has discovered the experience of unconditional love, whether they label it that or not. Even for the novice or the curious, an experience communicating with an animal opens vistas never before thought possible. In this manuscript, I have provided a comparison of the characteristics of both the animal and human mind. These are described in Table 1. Many spiritual seekers, including animal communicators, like myself have discovered that it is possible for humans to experience life on the transcendental level of the animal mind by adopting two tenets: first, abandon judgment, and second, abandon the concept of separateness. The truth is we are all one. These two modifications in thought result in the dissolution of the ego. We are not our egos. We are what the ego is hiding — spiritual beings — all made of the same stuff but in different forms. This is what separates the saints, avatars, gurus and sages from the rest of us. They realize this and operate from a position of love, unity, and compassion.

We humans are now ready for the next step in our evolution. It is what has been happening all over our globe, a giant leap in consciousness. Just as scientists now delve into the world of subparticles and nanobiological living systems, requiring a new way of looking at biological life and new paradigms, psychologists are delving into new worlds of mental awareness. Research like that of Valerie Hunt, Gary Schwartz and Linda Russek discovered that there is a way to measure the human aura and understand the afterlife. Television shows demonstrating inter-dimensional communication like that of John Edward and James Van Praagh, and inter-species communication with Sonja Fitzpatrick (Animal Planet's Pet Psychic), are making the supernatural realize itself as natural. What is really happening is that conscious awareness is breaking through former outdated taboos and superstitions and we are becoming connected with All That Is.

The pioneering work of David Bohm and Rupert Sheldrake have taught us that there is a background fabric of the universe made up of energy, and it provides for the manifestation of physical matter in all its myriad forms. Animals say this energy bond of attraction and attachment is made up of pure love. With the advent of the Internet, the world is becoming smaller and smaller. The Internet can be viewed as a manifestation of the universal mind in its most contemporary form. When one enters the telepathic field, there occurs a connection to a place in which a wealth of knowledge has been stored. The only requirement to access this knowledge is a quiet mind, an open heart, abandonment of judgment, and the illusion of separateness.

It is my hope that the story of my journey has touched your heart and has made you aware of the inner beauty of animals and all life. May you find your journey as pleasant.

Agnes Thomas

NOTES

Chapter Four
1.   Boone, (1954) p. 8.

Chapter Six
1.   Grey (1990).

Chapter Seven
1.   Schultz, (1975).
2.   Boone, (1980).

Chapter Eight
1.   Bohm, (1980).
2.   Chopra, (1996).
3.   Sheldrake, (1995).
4.   Sheldrake, (1999).
5.   McTaggert, (2002).
6.   Cathie, (1997).
7.   Grey, (1990).
8.   Grey, (2000).
9.   Boone, (1939).
10.   Boone, (1999).
11.   Boone, (1977).
12.   Boone, (1954) p.62.
13.   Schwartz, (1999).
14.   Schwartz, (2001).
15.   Schwartz, (2002).
16.   Hunt, (1996).
17.   Three Initiates, (1912) in the Kybalion.
18.   Hawkins, (2001).
19.   Schultz, (1975).
20.   Sheldrake, (1995).
21.   Sheldrake, (1996).

Chapter Nine
1.   Boone, (1954).
2.   Hunt, (1996).
3.   Brennan, (1988).
4.   Hunt, (1996).
5.   Virtue, (1977).
6.   Montgomery, (1982).

Chapter Eleven
1. Talbot, (1991).
2. Chopra, (2000)
3. Chopra, (2001).
4. Hunt, (1996).
5. Libet and Feinstein, cited in Talbot (1992) p.191.
6. Bohm, (1980).
7. Sheldrake, (1995).
8. Sheldrake, (1996).
9. Potts, (1984).
10. Schwartz, (2001).
11. Schwartz, (2001).
12. Poponin, (1995) p. 1.
13. Ibid, p. 2.
14. Sheldrake, (1999) p. 280.
15. Ibid, p. 167.

Chapter Twelve
1. Talbot, (1991).
2. Fox, (2000)
3. Grossman, (1999).
4. Emoto, (2004).

Chapter Thirteen
1. Thomas, (1992)

Chapter Fourteen
1. Swami Sri Yukteswar, quoted in Yogananda, (1992).
2. Thomas, (1982).
3. Archterberg and Siegal, cited in Talbot, (1991).
4. Gerber, (1988).
5. Perl, (2001).
6. Yogananda, (1994). p. 14

Chapter Fifteen
1. Yogananda, (1994).

REFERENCES

Bohm, David. Wholeness and the Implicate Order. Routledge & Kegan Paul, London, 1980.

Bohm, D. and Sheldrake, R. Morphogenetic fields and the implicate order. In R. Sheldrake. A New Science of Life. 2nd Ed. Blond, London, 1985.

Boone, J. Allen. Adventures in Kinship With All Life. Tree of Life Publications, Joshua Tree, CA, 1990.

Boone, J. Allen. Kinship With All Life. Harper, San Francisco, CA, 1954.

Boone, J. Allen. Letters To Strongheart. Prentice-Hall, Inc. New York 1939.

Boone, J. Allen. You Are The Adventure. Robert H. Sommer, Publisher, Harrington Park, NJ, 1977.

Brennan, Barbara Ann. Hands Of Light. Bantam books, div. of Bantam Doubleday Dell Publishing Group, Inc., New York, 1988.

Cathie, Bruce L. The Energy Grid: Harmonic 695 The Pulse of the Universe. Adventures Limited Press, Kempton, IL, 1997.

Chopra, Deepak. Creating Afflluence: Wealth Consciousness in the Field of All Possibilities. Eighth Edition. Buddy-Allen Publishing and New World Library, San Rafael, CA 1996.

Chopra, Deepak. The Conscious Universe (audiocassette). Hay House, Inc. 2000.

Chopra, Deepak. The Cosmic Mind and the Submanifest Order of Being (audiocassette), Hay House, Inc. 2001.

Emoto, Masaru. The Hidden Messages in Water. Beyond Words Publishing, Inc. 2004.

Fox, Matthew. One River, Many Wells. Penguin Putnam, Inc. New York, 2000.

Gerber, Richard. Vibrational Medicine. Bear Co, Santa Fe, NM, 1988.

Grey, Alex. Sacred Mirrors. Traditions International, Rochester, VT, 1990.

Grey, Alex. The Visionary Artist (tape). Sounds True, Boulder, CO, 2000.

Grossman, Warren. To Be Healed By The Earth. Seven Stories Press. New York, 1999.

Hawkins, David R. The Eye of the I: From which nothing is hidden. Veritas Publishing, Sedona, AZ, 2001.

Hunt, Valerie V. Infinite Mind: Science of the human vibrations of consciousness. Malibu Publishing, Malibu, CA,1996.

Libit, Benjamin, and Feinstein, Bertram. In: Talbot, Michael. The Holographic Universe. HarperPerrenial, New York, 1992, p. 191.

McTaggert, Lynne. The Field: The Quest for the Secret Force of the Universe. HarperCollins, New York, 2002.

Montgomery, Ruth. Strangers Among Us. Fawcett Crest, New York,1982.

Pearce, Joseph C. The Biology of Transcendence. Park Street Press, Rochester, VT, 2002.

Perl, Eric. The Reconnection. Jodere Group, Hay House, Carlsbad, CA, 2001.

Poponin, Vladimir. The DNA PHANTOM EFFECT: Direct Measurement of A New Field in the Vacuum Substructure. *Nanobiology: J. Res. Nanoscale Living Systems.* Vol 1(4), 1995.

Potts, Wayne K. The chorus line hypothesis of maneuver coordination in avian flocks. *Nature* 309:344-345, 1984.

Schultz, Duane. A History of Modern Psychology. 2nd ed. Academic Press, Inc. New York, 1975.

Schwartz, Gary E. The Afterlife Experiments. Atira Books, New York, 2002.

Schwartz, G. E., Rissel. L.G.S., Nelson, L.A., and Barentsen, C. Accuracy and Replicability of Anomalous After-Death Communication Across Highly Skilled Mediums. *J. Soc. Psychical Res.*, 65(1)no 282:1-25, 2001.

Schwartz, Gary E.R. and Russek, Linda G.S. The Living Energy Universe. Hampton Roads Publishing, Charlottesville, VA, 1999.

Shalain, Leonard. The Alphabet Versus The Goddess: The conflict between word and image. Putnam Penguin, Inc. 1999.

Sheldrake, Rupert. Dogs That Know When Their Owners Are Coming Home. Three Rivers Press, New York, 1999.

Sheldrake, Rupert. Seven Experiments That Could Change The World. Riverhead Books, div. Penguin Putnam, Inc. New York, 1995.

Swami Sri Yukteswar. In: Man's Eternal Quest. By Paramahansa Yogananda. Self-Realization Fellowship Internal Publications, Los Angeles, CA, 1992.

Talbot, Michael. The Holographic Universe. HarperPerennial, New York, 1991.

Thomas, Agnes J. Stimulation-Produced Analgesia and Suppression of Behavior in the Rat. Doctoral Dissertation, Case Western Reserve University, Cleveland, OH, 1982.

Thomas, Agnes J., Austin, William, Friedman, Lee, and Strohl, Kingman P. A model of ventilatory instability in the unrestrained rat. J. Appl. Physiol. 73(4):1530-1536, 1992.

Three Initiates. The Kybalian: Hermetic Philosophy. The Yogi Publication Society, Chicago, IL, 1912.

Virtue, Doreen. The Lightworker's Way. Hay House, Carlsbad, CA, 1997.

Yogananda, Paramahansa. The Quiet Mind: Sayings of White Eagle. White Eagle Publishing Trust, Hampshire, England, 15th Ed., 1994.

Contact Information About the Author

Consultations.

- Dr. Agnes Thomas can be reached through her website, *www. petstellthetruth.com*, or via e-mail at *talktopets@aol.com*. Consultations are by appointment only. The reader is asked to schedule an appointment by phone by calling (440)838-0911 before 8:00 p.m. Eastern StandardTime.

- Workshops in animal communication are listed on her website.

- Lectures and guest appearances by Dr. Agnes Thomas must be scheduled at least two months in advance.

- Ordering information. Copies of this book may be obtained from: *www.petstellthetruth.com*

Resources

Animal Communicators

Rebecca Richerson-Farris
461 Cheryl Avenue
White Rock, NM 87544
(505)672-1719
e-mail: *Wolfbecky@aol.com*

Vicka Lanier
P.O. Box 1013
Billings, MT 59103
www.helpyouheal.com

Sharon Orlando
10 Sheffield Station
Flemington, NJ 08822
(908)284-9160

Jacquelin Smith
5795 North Meadows Blvd. #B
Columbus, OH 43229
(614)436-8831
www.jacquelinsmith.com

Other resources

Mary Ellen "AngelScribe"
P.O. Box 1004
Cottage Grove, OR 97424
www.AngelScribe.com

Atira Hatton, Angelic Mystic
3935 S. 113th St.
Seattle, WA 98168
atira@actaccess.com

Linda LeColst
200 North Street #84
Danvers, MA 01923
www.SilverPersians.com

CPSIA information can be obtained at www.ICGtesting.com
Printed in the USA
LVOW092357110112

263499LV00003B/118/P

9 780980 241105